A PARENT'S GUIDE TO
EATING
DISORDERS
AND
OBESITY

THE CHILDREN'S HOSPITAL OF PHILADELPHIA

A PARENT'S GUIDE TO

EATING DISORDERS AND OBESITY

M A R T H A   M .   J A B L O W

Foreword by
C. EVERETT KOOP, M.D.

Delta

A Delta Book
Published by
Dell Publishing
a division of
Bantam Doubleday Dell Publishing Group, Inc.
666 Fifth Avenue
New York, New York 10103

Library of Congress Cataloging in Publication Data

Jablow, Martha Moraghan.
    A parent's guide to eating disorders and obesity/by Martha M.
Jablow.
        p.   cm.
    At head of title: The Children's Hospital of Philadelphia.
    Includes index and bibliographical references.
    ISBN 0-385-30030-1 (pbk.) : $10.00
    1. Eating disorders in children—Popular works.   2. Obesity in
children—Popular works.   I. Children's Hospital of Philadelphia.
II. Title.
RJ506.E18J33   1991
618.92'8526—dc20   91-15295
                                                                  CIP

Manufactured in the United States of America
Published simultaneously in Canada
January 1992

10 9 8 7 6 5 4 3 2 1

RRH

Contents

Foreword

A pleasant part of preparing this foreword concerns my ability to place the book in historical perspective. I was associated with The Children's Hospital of Philadelphia in the 1940s, when the late Irving J. Wolman, M.D., conducted pioneering studies on the digestibility of milk in infants. His work led to wide public acceptance of homogenized milk and recognition for his contribution two decades later. Dr. Wolman followed a long line of Children's Hospital's physicians who have made major advances in the knowledge we have about nutrition, including infant feeding and the eating habits of children, dating back to 1885.

It was a natural step to become further involved when the Hospital began to examine the role of nutrition in children with chronic diseases and eating disorders. An opportunity presented itself in 1970 to collaborate with the Philadelphia Child Guidance Clinic for an in-depth investigation of anorexia nervosa, a serious condition characterized by compulsive starvation and resultant hazardous loss of weight. The setting for this effort was Children's Hospital's Clinical Research Center (CRC), a special unit within the Hospital that permitted bedside and extensive laboratory research for ailments difficult to diagnose and difficult to treat. The director of the CRC, endocrinologist Lester Baker, M.D., worked closely with the Philadelphia Child Guidance Clinic's Director, Salvador Minuchin, M.D., who has been credited with the initial development of what is known as family-centered therapy or treatment of children within their families. The 1970 program represented a new modality for treatment that was to be the foundation for our management of other physical problems of childhood intertwined with children's emotional health problems.

Close collaboration of the two institutions has produced *Eating Disorders,* a book that helps parents understand what their child is going through if she or he is self-starving (anorexia nervosa), bingeing and purging (bulimia), or compulsively overeating. Readers will learn the danger signals of eating disorders, the medical complications that can arise from them, the psychological components of these problems, and how they can help their child recover. Most important, parents are encouraged to seek professional help early because these difficulties respond best when treated as soon as possible.

The media have covered anorexia nervosa and bulimia well. Many articles and programs have centered on celebrities who have had eating disorders, which are now increasing among American youth, although estimates of their rise vary widely. At the same time and perhaps paradoxically, our children have become heavier and less physically fit in the last two decades. These two trends may well be connected: overweight, sedentary young children grow up watching superthin actors and models on television, in movies, and in advertisements. By the time they are adolescents, they may turn to using food if they face other psychological dilemmas.

Parents are disturbed if they notice that one child is suddenly losing weight or another child begins to eat ravenously and secretly. They wonder if this is a "normal" aspect of development or if it could signal underlying psychological distress.

Any parent's best defense is information. Eating disorders and obesity are not matters of "simple willpower." Self-destructive eating behaviors are not the young person's fault and are not, therefore, something he or she can easily stop or change without extensive psychological help and support. Neither are they the parents' fault. Too often, parents are guilt-ridden about any abnormal childhood behavior. Readers will discover that this book is not concerned with laying blame at anyone's feet but with providing the information and guidance that is needed to help the child.

C. Everett Koop, M.D.
Surgeon-in-Chief Emeritus
The Children's Hospital of Philadelphia

Acknowledgments

The books in The Children's Hospital of Philadelphia series are intended to give parents access to current, accurate information about conditions and diseases affecting their children. In writing this book, I have been privileged to serve as a conduit for parents of young people with eating disorders. I have sat across physicians' desks and asked questions that you would undoubtedly ask and sought the guidance that you need to understand and help your child. Physicians at The Children's Hospital of Philadelphia and at the Philadelphia Child Guidance Clinic have shared their expertise with me during many hours of interviews. They reviewed my drafts and offered useful suggestions and clarifications. I have great respect for their professional knowledge and skill, and even more respect for them as caring human beings. Special appreciation goes to:

Robert I. Berkowitz, M.D., Director of the Adolescent

Weight Management Study at the Philadelphia Child Guidance Clinic and lecturer at the Department of Psychiatry of the University of Pennsylvania School of Medicine;

Bernice L. Rosman, Ph.D., Director of Education at the Philadelphia Child Guidance Clinic and Associate Clinical Professor at the Department of Psychiatry at the University of Pennsylvania School of Medicine;

John Sargent, M.D., Director of Child and Adolescent Psychiatry Training at the Philadelphia Child Guidance Clinic and Senior Physician at The Children's Hospital of Philadelphia;

Alberto C. Serrano, M.D., Medical Director of the Philadelphia Child Guidance Clinic; Psychiatrist-in-Chief and Director of the Psychiatry Division of The Children's Hospital of Philadelphia; Professor of Psychiatry and Pediatrics and Director of the Divison of Child and Adolescent Psychiatry in the Department of Psychiatry of the University of Pennsylvania School of Medicine;

Michael A. Silver, M.D., Medical Director of Inpatient Services at the Philadelphia Child Guidance Clinic; Assistant Physician at The Children's Hospital of Philadelphia; and Clinical Assistant Professor of Psychiatry and Pediatrics at the University of Pennsylvania School of Medicine;

Gail B. Slap, M.D., Director of Adolescent Medicine at The Children's Hospital of Philadelphia; Director of the Craig-Dalsimer Program, the Adolescent Medicine Section, General Internal Medicine, of the Hospital of the University of Pennsylvania; Associate Professor of Medicine in the Department of Medicine at the University of Pennsylvania School of Medicine; and

Virginia A. Stallings, M.D., Director of Nutrition Support Service at The Children's Hospital of Philadelphia and Assistant Professor of Pediatrics at the University of Pennsylvania School of Medicine.

I am most grateful to Shirley Bonnem, Vice President of The Children's Hospital of Philadelphia, and her assistant,

Dorothy Barnes, for their support and assistance throughout this project. Literary agent Nancy Love's guidance is equally appreciated. And Emily Reichert, Delacorte executive editor, has honed the book with clarity, grace, and enthusiasm.

Because this book is meant primarily for families, it could not have been written without the honest input of parents, brothers, sisters, and friends who have watched a beloved young person struggle daily with an eating disorder. In support-group sessions I attended, many families spoke with the utmost frankness about both their pain and their hope. By allowing me to listen to their heartfelt words, they expanded my understanding of eating disorders, which, I trust, has made this a richer book.

I appreciate the sage guidance and support of Pat Snyder, director of the Philadelphia chapter of the American Anorexia/Bulimia Association, and two of the chapter's group leaders: Lynne Kornblatt and Louise Quattrone Schlichter. Harin Feibish and Judith Stern, therapists who counsel people with eating problems, were also generous with their knowledge and insights. Professor Kelly D. Brownell, formerly co-director of the University of Pennsylvania's School of Medicine's Obesity Research Clinic, and now at Yale University, provided me with helpful information about obesity. And I appreciate the support of the two other authors of books in this series, Lisa J. Bain and Marion Steinmann.

Most important, I thank my husband Paul and my children, Cara and David, for their patience with me throughout this project.

–M.M.J.

Introduction

When the twentieth century dawned, Western culture equated fatness with well-being and prosperity. Consider the paintings of the day: Renoir's women were robust; Cassatt's children were plump; Pissarro's peasant women were broad-hipped and thick-armed as they raked hay at Eragny; Degas's dancers did not know the word *svelte.*

As the twenty-first century approaches, those pictures have been negated completely. Today's body is supposed to be thin and hard—fit, not fat. So says America's $33 billion weight-loss industry. Billboards promote dieting with illustrations of tape measures encircling twenty-two-inch waists. For those too self-conscious to join a fitness center or a group weight-loss program, television advertising makes it sound so easy: just dial an 800 number, and your very own personalized, computerized diet plan will arrive by mail so you can shed those dreadful pounds in the privacy of your own home.

Or if you prefer another method, you can even diet according to your astrological numbers.

Pity the poor Renoir model—she could never be today's cover girl. Imagine her, terry-cloth headband soaked by perspiration, as she works out on a treadmill to lose thirty pounds.

What happened to body image in the twentieth century? Both medicine and the media now tell us clearly that fat is out. Physicians remind us that we can decrease the risks of heart disease, cancer, hypertension, diabetes, and other conditions if we reduce our weight and exercise our muscles. We Americans have heard the message and are trying to do something about it. Sixty-five million of us—about half the women and one-quarter of the men in the United States—are dieting. We are cutting our calories, often by keeping an estimated thirteen thousand weight-control services in business across the country. But in truth, we are not doing it for our health alone. The fashion, diet, and fitness industries pitch an enticing message: We will be happier people if we look good, and looking good means looking thinner.

Our children grow up watching us watch our weight, watching television ads for diet products, and watching slender ballerinas, gymnasts, and fashion models. The thin-is-better message has become so pervasive in contemporary culture that it reaches deep into early childhood. When a group of preschoolers were surveyed about their body image preferences, they were offered two dolls with the same hair, facial features, and clothing. The dolls were identical except for the fact that one was thin and the other was fat. The children— including the chubby ones—overwhelmingly chose the thin doll.

Yet two dangerous facts have emerged as our culture leans toward a thinner and thinner ideal: the obesity rate among American children has doubled in the last twenty years, while the incidence of anorexia nervosa and bulimia has grown among adolescents and young adults to the point where the word *epidemic* is sometimes applied to their rise. Are these two trends linked? Perhaps not clearly or directly, but some doctors who treat both eating disorders and childhood obesity are concerned that the ascending obesity rate and our culture's ever-increasing pressure to be thin could lead to even more anorexia and bulimia as girls and young women try to reduce their weight by choosing unhealthy, excessive methods. Young people who develop eating disorders often do not start out as overweight, but their concern that they will become obese in a society that worships slimness may trigger harmful dieting or a binge-purge cycle, especially if particular psychological factors in their lives are in place.

It is essential to understand from the outset that anorexia, bulimia, and compulsive overeating *are not solely about food or weight or body size,* though they may appear to be on the surface. Eating disorders never exist in a vacuum. They are intricately bound up in a knot of inner conflicts. Eating disorders are about focusing on food as a means to control, survive, or cope with the multitude of psychological dilemmas that face adolescents and young adults. Eating disorders are about feelings, about forging an identity as a young person, about low self-esteem, about the confusing paradox of loving and hating your family simultaneously, about emerging sexuality, and, in some cases, about sexual abuse in childhood.

As parents of a child who has an eating disorder or who is seriously overweight, you are undoubtedly concerned about both your child's physical and emotional health. If your child is obese (20 percent or more above his ideal body weight for age, height, and gender) you have grave concerns about his becoming an obese adult, not to mention the daily slings and arrows his psyche suffers as a fat child among peers who scorn fat children. You have watched helplessly as your child dissolves in tears when called "Blimp," or "Fat Albert," or "Lard Butt" by other children. You feel angry at those children and frustrated with all the unsuccessful efforts you and your child have made to reduce his weight.

Obesity per se is not considered an eating disorder by the American Psychiatric Association, which has formulated definitions for diagnosing anorexia and bulimia. And while there is no evidence that obese people are more or less psychologically ill than the normal-weight population, many physicians consider childhood obesity a serious physical and psychological concern. Therefore, Chapter 7 offers information about childhood obesity and suggestions for treating your child's weight while also promoting his emotional well-being. Chapters 8 and 9 deal primarily with psychotherapy for anorexia and bulimia, but the information contained in those chapters can also benefit parents of obese children who have psychological dilemmas related to their weight.

If you suspect—or have already discovered—that your child has an eating disorder, you are undoubtedly distraught. You are confused and frightened when you see your child starving or stuffing herself. Perhaps you have found a surprisingly large stash of laxatives in her drawers when you put clean laundry in her room. You feel deceived and angry when you frequently overhear her vomit soon after a meal; but when you ask her about it, she denies that anything is wrong.

If she is losing so much weight that you can nearly see her skeleton, you feel guilt, frustration, anguish, and probably rage. "Why the hell don't you just eat!" you scream at her when she spends a half-hour pushing two tiny pieces of meat around her dinner plate and nibbling only a salad. You feel like a failure as a parent because no matter what you try, no matter how hard you have tried, you cannot change her abnormal eating behavior. She seems to be self-destructing before your eyes, and you simply cannot understand why she is doing this to herself and to your family.

In this book you will meet Sheila, Jackie, and Debby, each a composite of many young people who exhibit eating disorders. And you will meet Robert, a composite of obese youths.

These adolescents illustrate the commonalities of young people with anorexia, bulimia, compulsive overeating, and obesity. You may recognize in them characteristics and behaviors similar to those of your child. But please keep in mind that your child is truly unique. She may have some or many of the *characteristics* of an eating disorder but she *is not* that eating disorder. She is first and foremost a young person acting in a certain way. She has her own reasons for behaving this way, her own unique problems with how she acts, and her own unique rewards for her behavior. We hope that this book will help you to understand that anorexia, bulimia, and compulsive overeating differ for each individual. The most important key to this understanding is the person—your daughter —not the symptoms of her disorder. The point is not to match your child, detail by detail, with the youths depicted here, but to give you basic information by which you can recognize your child's disorder, understand its ramifications, and deal with its treatment.

Based on the experiences of physicians, psychotherapists, patients, and families at The Children's Hospital of Philadelphia and its psychiatric affiliate, the Philadelphia Child Guidance Clinic, this book discusses common patterns that predominate in families whose child has an eating disorder, and it suggests treatment options. We promise no quick fix, no magic pill. These are complex situations that are often long-term and costly to remedy. But they *can* be treated. And the sooner eating disorders are recognized, the more readily they are treated. No blame will be placed in your lap; rather, we will suggest to you alternative ways of relating to your child in order to help her become an independent, competent young person who develops healthier ways of living than self-starving or bingeing and purging.

You may be tempted to skip over some of the chapters. If you know your child has anorexia, for example, you may think that the chapter on compulsive overeating is irrelevant to you. But we urge you to read every chapter because many threads weave through these various disorders and your understanding will be greater if you learn about all of them.

While this book is intended primarily for parents, you may wish to share it with your child's friends, teachers, siblings, and grandparents. She can only benefit from the understanding and support of those who are important in her life.

AUTHOR'S NOTE Eating disorders occur far more frequently among females than among males, although the incidence among males appears to be increasing. To solve every writer's he/she dilemma, I have chosen to use mainly feminine pronouns throughout this book simply because the vast majority of young people with eating disorders are still female.

CHAPTER 1

Profiles of Three Young Women with Eating Disorders

The girls shift nervously in their hard plastic chairs. Sheila twists a strand of long tawny hair. Jackie crosses, uncrosses, and recrosses her ankles. Debby folds and unfolds her arms across her stomach. Today is the first time they have come to a support-group meeting for adolescents and young adults with eating disorders. Each could not be any more anxious and uncomfortable.

Sheila, fourteen years old, immediately sizes up who has been coming to these meetings for months. They are the more confident ones—the talkers, she decides. She is curious about them, especially the ones who admit they have an eating disorder—because Sheila is positive that she does not. She only came to this meeting because her parents insisted on it. Sheila vowed to herself that she would not say a word. "Okay, I'll go, Mom," she promised as her mother practically pushed her through the door. "I'll go and listen, if it makes you happy. But I really don't have a problem, you know. I don't have a huge appetite, and I just don't want to get fatter."

Eighteen-year-old Jackie slumps in her chair and will not look in the direction of the group leader. If she makes eye contact, Jackie knows, she may be called on to comment. This is the last place she wants to be, but somehow she knows that she really needed to come. When her roommate suggested that she go to the group, Jackie was almost grateful for the excuse to go.

Debby, sixteen, hates being in this room. She has felt claustrophobic ever since the door closed and the group leader introduced herself. Debby surveys the others in the room. Only two of the twenty young people sitting in the circle of chairs are young men. She notices that most of the girls seem to be of average weight, but a few look extremely skinny and pale. She wishes she could be that thin. Then she tunes out the conversation around her and thinks about the diner she passed as she walked from the bus stop to this building. *"As soon as I get out of here . . ."* Debby cannot stop thinking of the foods she will order after the meeting.

Sheila, Jackie, and Debby have serious eating disorders that hold them prisoners of various forms of psychological distress and that threaten to endanger their physical health. Each girl is confused by her eating disorder—she both hates the disorder and loves it. Just as she clung to her beloved stuffed animal when she was very young, she cannot just "give it up," as her family and friends have urged. She cannot simply let it go. It is not a matter of willpower. It is not a matter of food or hunger. Rather, her eating disorder is tied up with her feelings about herself and her family. She feels inadequate: "I'm not good enough."

She cannot quite sort out her emotions, but she knows that, when she has certain feelings, binge eating or rigorously abstaining from food helps her cope—at least for a while. She often does not like herself the way she is, yet she cannot find a way to change. And sometimes she is not sure she even *wants* to change because her eating disorder is a survival mechanism, a way of protecting herself and adapting to distress.

Sheila has been anorectic for nearly a year. She is five feet, five inches tall, and her weight has dropped steadily over the past ten months from 120 to 86 pounds. Sheila firmly believes that she is still too fat, and she exercises vigorously every day, sometimes twice a day. To conceal her skin-and-bones frame and to retain her body heat even in summer, she wears layers of baggy sweaters or sweatsuits.

The group discussion is centering on food likes and dislikes when the group leader turns to Sheila and gently asks what she normally eats during the course of a typical day.

"Um, for breakfast, I usually have a piece of dry toast—the light, 40-calorie-a-slice kind, without butter or margarine, and some tea. I hate the school lunches, so I take a container of yogurt to school. And for dinner—well, my family likes us all to eat together, but they eat a lot of heavy meat-and-potatoes stuff, so I just have small portions of that and a big salad. It's plenty for me, really. I like my diet, and I feel fine," she answers hesitantly.

Sheila does not tell them that her father recently began yelling at her to eat "at least three pieces of meat" or that she has mastered the trick of putting the fork to her mouth, pretending to chew and swallow, then stuffing the meat in her paper napkin, to be thrown out later, unbeknownst to her parents. She feels good about deceiving them, actually. Staying on her strict self-imposed diet has made her feel good for the first time in her life. She is proud of herself, proud of her self-control, she is thinking to herself, when someone across the room speaks up:

"I used to do that—just eat a salad at dinner. I felt pretty virtuous about it, too," the young woman says. "But what

I'm learning in therapy, about myself and my family, is that I'm sort of a control freak."

Sheila listens intently.

"By sitting there with my family, just eating one little lettuce leaf at a time," the other girl says, "I was really trying to show my parents that there was something I could control—my food, what went into my own body, my weight—because they've been trying to control me all my life. My mother's always telling me how I'm supposed to feel, act, dress. When I was little, she talked about what *we* would do, or what *we* would like. She never asked me how *I* felt or what *I* wanted to do. It was like she was living my life for me, like I was a marionette and she was working the strings. Like, Mother-knows-best. Oh, don't get me wrong—I love my mother. But I'm starting to see how anorexia became my way of taking some control for myself and cutting those strings that tied me to her."

Jackie is also listening closely. *"I wish I had some control,"* she thinks. *"I'm such an out-of-control pig, stuffing my face whenever I'm unhappy or stressed out. And then I run to the toilet to vomit it up. Sometimes I think I look into the toilet bowl more than I look into the mirror. But I sure don't want to stop."*

Jackie is a freshman in college and has been bulimic for three years. She began—innocently enough, she thought—by secretly bingeing once every two or three months, usually right after some upsetting event at home or in school. While her family slept, she gobbled sweet foods so quickly that she hardly chewed. She hated the bingeing, hated sneaking food from the kitchen cupboards and freezer. Terrified of being caught, she often thought of herself as a thief in the night.

She had heard that it was easy to make herself vomit after a binge by sticking a finger down her throat and gagging. It was awful at first, but Jackie soon discovered that it made her feel good. She felt comforted, almost numbed. As her binges grew more frequent—she now averages three or four a week —she perfected the technique of constricting her abdominal muscles in order to vomit, so she does not need to stick her finger down her throat anymore. She has tried diet pills and laxatives to relieve the bloated feeling, but she prefers vomiting.

Jackie is five feet, three inches tall and weighs 135—not obese by any medical standard, but she believes that she is grossly overweight. Her weight often fluctuates over a ten-pound swing. Her fear of being fat so dominates her life that the bathroom scale has become her horoscope. When she steps on the scale each morning, the digital number staring back at her convinces her this will either be a good day or a bad day. One pound more than yesterday = bad. One pound less = good.

Debby is a compulsive overeater and is medically obese at five feet, four inches tall and 178 pounds. (The medical definition of *obese* is more than 20 percent above one's ideal body weight based on height, age, and gender. Please see pages 92–93 for further discussion of ideal body weight.) Debby's ideal body weight is 120. She binges, but unlike Jackie, she does not purge. Her friends and family are baffled by her high weight because she eats very little in front of them, and she is always talking about the latest diet she is trying to follow. Her weight is the central focus of her life. Debby will not go to school dances, and she refuses to swim or participate in many other physical activities because she is so embarrassed by her weight. She frequently fantasizes about being thin.

When someone in the support group speaks of "becoming a better person when I finally get thin," Debby's attention is captured. "That's what I'm always telling myself, too," she hears herself say aloud.

As the support group proceeds, Sheila, Jackie, and Debby are gradually drawn into the discussion. They listen more than they speak, but by the end of the hour, each has moved a step closer to understanding the particular eating behavior that she thought, until now, she alone possessed.

"I can't believe that some of you do the same things I've been doing, stuff my family doesn't even know I do—like wolfing down frozen pizza and a half-gallon of ice cream at one in the morning!" Jackie exclaims. "I thought I was the world's only secret eater!"

"And I thought I was the only one who cut her food into tiny pieces and made them into little patterns on my plate," adds Sheila, despite herself.

"We've talked a lot about what we eat or don't eat," the group leader says, "but we've learned that anorexia and bulimia and compulsive overeating are really about our feelings, not about food and weight. We get hung up on food and body size, but what's underneath all this? Now that we know we're not the only self-starvers or binge-purgers in the world, let's think about the occasions when we do these things and why and how we feel when we do them."

"I know now that I'm anorectic, but I denied it for a really long time," remarks one of the older girls. "I've been in therapy for a while—sometimes my parents come along to the sessions—and it's still hard for me to understand. I love my parents, and when I don't eat and keep losing weight, I know it upsets them. But I still want to keep doing it. They say I'm destructive, that I'm destroying myself and our family. But I don't mean to."

"Self-destruction is not intentional," the group leader explains. "When parents and friends ask you, 'Why are you doing this to yourself? Why are you risking your health?' they need to understand—and we need to understand—that eating disorders are a way we try to feel better about ourselves, a way we help ourselves function in a world that threatens or upsets us. It's hard for parents to see that, when all they see on the outside is an anorectic girl who's eating only 300 or 400 calories a day and whose weight seems to drop every week, or a bulimic girl who's emptying the pantry shelves and maybe stealing money from Mom's purse to buy out the 7-Eleven's supply of chips and candy bars and cookies. But we all have to understand that this destructiveness—and it *is* taking a tremendous destructive toll, emotionally and physically—is a by-product of our problem."

The group leader goes on to explain that many people with eating disorders initially deny their problems. "Now some of you, especially those who are anorectic, probably won't agree that your eating behaviors are destructive. Many anorectic girls come to this group, and from the moment they walk through the door, they deny that they have any problem or that they're hurting themselves. They truly believe that they're in control of their weight. They hold on to that anorexia because it gives them a great sense of power—you feel competent, proud of yourself. It boosts your self-esteem because sticking to those rigid rules you've set for yourselves—so many hours of exercise a day, only so many calories, only certain foods eaten in a certain pattern—makes you feel strong and powerful."

But, the group leader continues, there are healthier ways of controlling problems. "What we learn from each other in this group, and what I hope you're discovering with your families in psychotherapy sessions, are new and better ways of coping with your problems. It takes a long time to come to grips with that, but those of us who have been through it can tell you that your eating disorder won't go away through willpower, or just by putting on twenty pounds if you're anorectic or by losing twenty pounds if you're overweight. The key is to understand our emotions and our relationships with our families. After we begin to understand those, we can find healthier ways of growing up and more constructive ways of living.

"The most important message you're getting in therapy, I hope, is that each of us is capable of change," she says. "We don't have to live with the anxiety and panic and fear that accompany our eating disorders. That may be hard for some of us to believe right now because a big part of an eating disorder is the feeling that things won't change, that we're trapped forever in our personal circumstances. Maybe some of us don't *want* to change because this way we feel somehow in control, and any change seems frightening. But we can change and recover with the help of therapists, our families, time, and a willingness to be uncomfortable at times. I'm glad you came today, and I hope you come back to our next meeting."

As the meeting ends, several participants pick up literature about eating disorders from a nearby table. Few speak to one another. As each girl goes home, her head spins with replayed snatches of conversation of the group.

Debby stops by the diner and orders a piece of lemon meringue pie and coffee. As she stirs in three spoons of sugar and stares into the steaming coffee, she thinks that maybe she *will* talk with her parents about finding a counselor or nutritionist who can help her get to the source of her compulsive eating. *"Enough of these on-again-off-again diets,"* she tells herself. *"All my life they haven't worked. I need more than just another weight-loss gimmick, I guess."*

Before Jackie reaches the bus for a ride back to campus, she stops by a clothing store with a "sale" sign in the window. While looking through a rack of shirts, Jackie recognizes a girl who had just been at the support-group meeting. The girl is talking with a heavy woman as they look at the jeans.

"These would look nice on you, dear," the woman says as she pulls out a full-cut pair of acid-washed jeans.

"Oh, no, Mom, they wouldn't show my figure," the girl responds.

Jackie leaves the store wondering about that girl and her mother. The girl had said little in the discussion group except that she is fifteen and does not want to get fat, though she appears to be average size. *"Must not want to get fat like her mother,"* Jackie guesses. *"She probably binges and purges just like me. Yeah, I was about her age when I started. At first it was like an experiment, and I thought I could control it. Now it controls me.''*

That night, Jackie calls home to tell her parents that she is bulimic and that she is going to try to get help through the college health center. Her parents are so shocked that they can barely speak—a rare occasion in a family that usually throws words around with abandon.

Sheila goes home to a wide-eyed mother.

"How was the group, honey?" she asks tentatively.

"Okay, but it's not for me. Those girls really have problems. But I don't. I don't need to go back next time." Sheila goes to her room and changes into her running shoes for her daily four-mile run.

While she is out, her parents replay an all-too-frequent argument. "You've *got* to make her eat! You can *see* how thin she's gotten. Her hair has lost its luster, her ribs practically stick through her blouses! I can't sit through another meal and watch her play with her food, push it all around her plate, and not eat it!" her father exclaims.

"I know, I know. I've tried talking to her, but she has this nearly religious commitment to her so-called diet," Sheila's mother says. "I thought that if she went to this support group today, it might help, but I guess it didn't."

"Well, you're the one who thinks she's anorectic. I don't know about that, but I *do* think we've got to get her to a doctor. This is certainly no ordinary diet she's on."

"I've tried convincing her of that, but it just upsets her, and I'm afraid of upsetting her anymore."

"So what are you going to do?"

"Me? Why is it that *I* always have to do something when it comes to Sheila?"

"Because you're her mother. She's close to you. I don't know how to deal with her. Especially when she's so irrational about food and exercising. What's happened to her, anyway? She was always such a sweet, obedient girl until recently."

"I don't know. But I stay awake at night wondering the same thing. Can this be our wonderful daughter—the prettiest, smartest, most loving daughter any mother would want? She gets good grades, has nice friends, never has been in any trouble—I am completely puzzled."

CHAPTER 2

Understanding Eating Disorders

What are eating disorders? Where do they come from? How do they begin? Are they new to our culture? To someone who does not have an eating disorder, these behaviors appear to be bizarre and frightening. How does a parent begin to understand them?

From this chapter through Chapter 6, we will specifically discuss anorexia, bulimia, and compulsive overeating, but a basic understanding must begin here: *Eating disorders develop when food and weight become the obsessive focus for unmet psychological needs.*

THE FOCUS ON FOOD

Why does food become the central focus of a person's life instead of something else? Isn't food simply food—material to fuel our bodies? Yes and no. If we look beyond our personal view of food for a moment, we see that our culture embellishes food with other meanings—some subtle, some not so subtle:

FOOD CAN MEAN LOVE. When a parent says, "I made this delicious dinner—your favorite foods—just for you," isn't that an expression of love?

FOOD CAN MEAN CONNECTION. Bonding starts the day a child is born. Holding her newborn in her arms, a mother gives sustenance by nursing or offering a bottle. She looks into her baby's eyes, and the infant gazes back at her face. The baby comes to recognize her as a separate, distinct person, yet one on whom the infant is totally dependent. And when is this first human relationship forged? While feeding.

FOOD CAN MEAN COMFORT. When a child falls off a bike and skins a knee, what does Mommy do after cleaning and bandaging the scrape? She may offer milk and cookies. When feelings are hurt by an unkind classmate, perhaps she buys her child an ice cream cone after school. When he stays home, confined to bed with a virus, she offers hot soup. Or if the child's stomach is upset, she may fix vanilla ice cream floating in a tall glass of ginger ale.

The concept of food as maternal comfort has become such an integral part of contemporary culture that savvy merchandisers even cash in on it: a bakery cleverly markets "Magic Mommy" brownies. How could a sad, upset, or stressed-out consumer possibly resist "Magic Mommy" brownies in the bakeshop window? Just as he turned to Mommy and her comforting food when he was a child—for love, for strokes, or for company when he felt alone—he may well turn to food as an adult, or so the bakery owner hopes.

Another example of how food associations can grow to unusual proportions in a person's life is Jackie's bulimic use of food as comfort. In therapy, Jackie is now learning to recognize that she binges when she is under particular stress. At those times, food comforts her emotional needs. When she is feeling bad about herself, unloved and unworthy, she stuffs herself to fill an emptiness that is not physical. She is not even cognizant of whether she is actually hungry. Rather, she gorges to fill her emotional emptiness and to push down the torments that make her feel out of control. The binge, followed by vomiting, lets her have her cake and eat it, too—quite literally. The binge smothers her emotional cries, while the purge comforts her by convincing her that all the food she has eaten will not turn to fat because she has regurgitated it. Jackie manages her psychological pain by smothering her emotional needs with gobs of food, then regains some "control" by purging. A number of bulimics say that the purge gives them more than a clean slate for their guilt feelings about bingeing; it also soothes them with a numbness that feels physical, a sense of cleansing, of relieving the bloating caused by the binge. If you have ever vomited when you were ill, you have probably experienced a similar sense of "feeling better" afterward.

FOOD CAN MEAN PLEASURE AND ENTERTAINMENT. How do adults celebrate an anniversary, a job promotion, or simply a pleasant Saturday night after a hectic week? With a slow-paced, candlelit dinner at a fine restaurant. Children also grow up associating food with celebrations and joyful events: birthday cakes, pizza parties, and elaborate meals at Thanksgiving or religious holidays.

There is nothing wrong with this. Good food and relaxed meals should be enjoyed. But in an eating disorder, the normal associations made with food are stretched to the point where food takes on an obsessive pull. When a mother says, "I made this delicious dinner just for you," she may be expressing more than love. The child may perceive her intent as trying to control her, some psychologists believe. The message the child hears (whether that is the mother's real meaning or not) may be, "Love me back. I made this special dinner so you'll love me. Eat it to show me that you love me." The child could interpret this as "Mom is trying to control me, to smother me with her love." The child wants and needs Mother's love, but she also thirsts for some autonomy. The child grows up confused by this mixed message: "I know she loves me, but if she really loved me, she wouldn't make me prove I love her back by eating this meal."

THE FOCUS ON WEIGHT

Like food, weight also becomes an obsessive focus for the unmet psychological needs of someone with an eating disorder. Weight is directly related to food, of course. But in the context of eating disorders, weight is more than simply the result of the food one ingests and does or does not expend in burned calories. Weight also connotes one's size and body image. As we did with food, we need to look beyond weight's immediate, obvious meaning to understand how and why it takes on an obsessive quality in eating disorders.

It is helpful to begin by examining the role of weight in our society and its meaning to our concept of ourselves individually. Throughout the twentieth century, a woman's weight has been compared to a standard set by fashion and the visual media—particularly movies, television, and advertising. In the 1920s, flappers turned the formerly buxom female standard into a flat-chested, skinny one. In the thirties and forties, the "perfect-size" woman was allowed to put on a few pounds as Americans pulled out of the Depression and money and food were more plentiful. By the 1950s, a full figure like that of Marilyn Monroe, Jayne Mansfield, or Esther Williams had become the ideal. But in the 1960s, like so many other aspects of that watershed decade, body image changed yet again. Thin became in. Most female singers, actresses, and models were built like Twiggy or Jane Fonda—or they tried to be.

Cultural trends swing high and low, and most are harmless.

But when a young woman who has unmet psychological needs and whose self-image is emerging precariously lives in a society that bombards her with subliminal and overt messages like "be thin = be happy = be sexy = be important," she absorbs the message quite literally.

Sheila is such a young woman. Emphasis on weight has prevailed in her home for as long as she can remember. Her mother and older sister work hard to stay slim by dieting and exercise. They own five different exercise videotapes. When Sheila was younger, she worried that she would never be as attractive (read "thin") as her sister or her mother. Her mother was always pushing fruit for dessert instead of the ice cream or pastry she was offered at friends' homes. Fashion magazines jammed her family's mailbox. Without even asking if Sheila wanted them, her mother took out subscriptions to *Seventeen* and *Glamour* for her when she was twelve. Since their toddler days, an overweight cousin was held up to Sheila as a warning flag whenever she wanted a second helping. The cousin was always mentioned in the context of "too bad she's so overweight; she has such a pretty face; if only she were thin, she'd be popular." Sheila's mother and sister are hardly the only women in America who are weight conscious. They simply have bought the media message and have taken it home, where they pass it on to Sheila.

This is certainly not to imply that a society that deifies thinness *causes* eating disorders. But it does cultivate an extremely fertile field where the seeds of a vulnerable young woman's emotional needs can develop into an eating disorder. If she grows up hearing and accepting the message that she must be thin to be attractive, happy, and accepted, her emotional needs can take root in that message. They can grow into an eating disorder that becomes her way of filling her needs with obsessions about her food and weight. For a young woman in a society where thinness has become a cult, and in a world where she rarely has had the experience of controlling anything, controlling her own weight and the size of her body becomes her means of grabbing control. She may be growing up, like Sheila, in a family that exerts so much control over her feelings and behaviors that she has virtually no autonomy. Or she may be living in an environment where there is so much ambiguity, even chaos, that there is a constant sense of everything being out of control.

AN HISTORICAL PERSPECTIVE ON ANOREXIA

In the past twenty years, reams of information have appeared in the popular media about anorexia and bulimia. Pat Boone's daughter, Cherry Boone O'Neill, wrote a painfully honest book, *Starving for Attention,* about her decade of anorexia and her subsequent recovery. Former gymnast Cathy Rigby McCoy has spoken frankly about her bulimia. Jane Fonda went through a bulimic period during college and her early years as an actress. Pop singer Karen Carpenter died of complications of anorexia nervosa in 1983 at the age of thirty-two. While such celebrity disclosures brought eating disorders into the open and helped to educate the public about these previously little-known phenomena, it would be inaccurate to think that anorexia and bulimia suddenly sprang up in the late twentieth century.

Though the term *anorexia nervosa* first entered the medical literature a century ago, some of its symptoms had been noted for centuries. Historians find references to anorectic behaviors as far back as A.D. 895, when a serf named Friderada, who apparently became so disgusted by food after gorging, started to fast rigidly. Like some modern anorectics, she ate a little secretly; she was highly industrious, denied her starving state, and refused help.'

Friderada was also extremely pious—a trait that appears in the behaviors of medieval women who starved because they believed they would become more virtuous in the sight of God if they mortified their bodies. These ascetics were often rebellious young women who came from patriarchal families and who reacted to strict social morality and Church authority. In their battle to conquer their bodies through a rigorous spiritual regimen, they defied religious officials and their families by refusing to eat, going without sleep, suffering extremes of heat and cold, and working or walking strenuously —all to mortify the flesh and purify the spirit. Joan of Arc is believed to have been anorectic, and Saint Catherine of Siena supposedly lived on a spoonful of herbs a day. When she was forced to eat, she put twigs down her throat to bring up the food. By the seventeenth and eighteenth centuries, a few physicians began to call such food abstinence *anorexia mirabilis,* meaning a miraculously inspired loss of appetite. Stories about the "miraculous maids" who apparently lived without eating were translated and spread as printing became common throughout Europe. According to Joan Jacobs Brumberg, author of *Fasting Girls,* their stories evolved into a popular folk tradition between the sixteenth and the eighteenth centuries in both Protestant and Catholic countries. In 1600 a French doctor, Jacob Viverius, observed fourteen-year-old Jane Balan, who claimed to have eaten and drunk nothing for three years. After examining her emaciated body and finding no evidence of feces or urine to indicate food intake, Viverius concluded that Jane must be a miraculous maid whose life was sustained only by God.

But others were not so convinced by supernatural explanations. Clergy and physicians scrutinized these self-starving girls to determine whether their abstinence was authentic. When a sixteenth-century "miraculous maid" in Germany was caught eating on the sly, she was executed. The English philosopher and rationalist Thomas Hobbes met a young woman whose "belly touches her backbone" after six months of fasting in 1668. Though she was considered a saint by her townsfolk, she was "manifestly sick," in Hobbes's view. In 1694, the physician Richard Morton described in a "treatise on consumptions" the cases of two sad, anxious adolescents who had symptoms similar to what we call anorexia today.

One was a girl who resembled "a skeleton only clad in skin" but who did not appear to have a fever or the respiratory symptoms associated with consumption. Some medical historians have credited Morton with the "discovery" of anorexia nervosa because of these descriptions, but others disagree because Morton also described other symptoms, such as periodic fainting fits, that are not part of the contemporary diagnosis.

On this side of the Atlantic, Puritans like Cotton Mather followed scientific developments in Europe and drew parallels to Massachusetts witchcraft. Mather concluded that extended fasting was "strangely agreeable" to so-called witches like Margaret Rule, who was assaulted as she fasted by eight "cruel specters" sent by the Devil himself.

By the nineteenth century, the term *fasting girl* entered European and American lexicons to describe a girl's food refusal when her intention was ambiguous and not necessarily spiritual. Victorians thought some of these girls were "hysterical" or particularly prone to nervous disorders, while others were thought to be ascetics seeking transcendence over the material body in much the same vein as Spiritualism, a late-nineteenth-century fascination. Living obscurely on the English moors, nineteenth-century novelist Emily Brontë may not only have been anorectic herself, a recent biography suggests, but may also have given anorectic qualities to Catherine, her heroine in *Wuthering Heights.*

Fasting girls in Great Britain and the United States drew wide public attention in newspapers of the day. One of the most famous, Mollie Fancher of Brooklyn, became such a celebrity that P. T. Barnum tried to recruit her for his traveling circus.

While the press was having a heyday with fasting girls' stories, it took nineteenth-century medicine to transform self-starvation from an act of personal piety to a disease symptom, bringing it from the religious sphere to the secular. In the field of medicine, the nineteenth century is noted for identifying and classifying many diseases for the first time. For most of the nineteenth century, anorexia or "absence of appetite," as defined in an 1865 medical dictionary, was considered part of any number of other conditions: a symptom of stomach diseases, tuberculosis, cancer, even the nausea of pregnancy. But in the 1870s anorexia came into its own as a new and independent disease. Almost simultaneously in 1873, Sir William Gull in England and Charles Lasegue in France described a set of symptoms: the refusal to eat, severe weight loss, constipation, amenorrhea (the absence or suppression of menstruation), low body temperature, low pulse rate, and passion for exercise. As they defined it, anorexia was primarily a noneating behavior accompanied by a number of physical symptoms. But while Gull looked at anorexia with a medical focus—saying that the condition involved what he called "simple starvation" and no organic disease—Lasegue emphasized the psychological aspects. He explained the mental stages through which a patient and family pass during the course of the disease. Lasegue described an anorectic girl as typically between the ages of fifteen and twenty and attributed her anorexia to an "emotional cause" that she might either acknowledge or hide. Lasegue was the first to link a patient's symptoms to her family interactions. He noted that any description of anorectics "would be incomplete without reference to their home life. Both the patient and her family form a tightly knit whole, and we obtain a false picture of the disease if we limit our observation to the patients alone."[2] In these families, he pointed out, emotional demands were often expressed around food issues.

After Gull and Lasegue's publications, the medical literature began to mention other cases of anorexia. But how were doctors to treat it? Frequently in the late nineteenth century and into the early twentieth, the suggested cure was removal of the girl from her family environment where she would rest and be seen only by a doctor and nurse until she regained weight.

In the early twentieth century, anorexia came to be seen as a deep psychological disturbance, often resistant to treatment. In the 1940s, psychoanalysts tried to explain anorexia in terms of unconscious fantasies and aversion to sexuality. By the 1960s, the body of eating-disorder literature began to mushroom, and in the 1970s, the focus shifted to the family as the crucible of anorexia. In the 1970s and 1980s, the fact that eating disorders do not exist in a cultural vacuum had made a strong impact. Not only were family interactions examined, but many feminists also began to look at the links between eating disorders and women's cultural and political roles. In recent years, too, biobehaviorists have been searching for neuroendocrine changes and genetic/physiological signs of vulnerability to eating disorders.

In 1980, the American Psychiatric Association published diagnostic definitions and descriptions of eating disorders in its *Diagnostic and Statistical Manual of Mental Disorders III* (known as *DSM-III*) and revised and updated them in 1987 *(DSM-III-R)*. These diagnostic criteria for anorexia will be discussed in Chapter 4 and those for bulimia in Chapter 5.

An Historical Perspective on Bulimia

Bulimia does not have as detailed a history in the medical literature as anorexia, but it was recognized as long ago as the second century A.D. Although the word *bulimia* comes from the Greek, meaning "great hunger," that definition ignores the flip side of bingeing—that is, purging.

The ancient physician Galen, who has been called the father of experimental physiology and second only to Hippocrates in the history of medicine, called the disease *bulimis* in the second century A.D. An acidic humor in the stomach was thought to cause it by producing false signals of hunger. *Bulimia* or *boulimie* popped up in medical literature sporadically, and in France in the nineteenth century, it was linked to diabetes. But bulimia received far less recognition than anorexia until recently. For example, many college students in the 1960s can recall at least one fellow student who binged and then vomited in the dormitories of that era. They knew that the student had a problem, that what she was doing was unhealthy and not simply a new quirky diet, but few knew it had a name and most had no clue as to its cause. Today's college generation knows the name *bulimia* as well as *anorexia,* and almost everyone has heard about or personally knows a young person who has been or is bulimic or anorectic. But there is still a heavy aura of secrecy around eating disorders and a hesitancy to discuss them.

THE PREVALENCE AMONG FEMALES

Why do eating disorders occur primarily among young women? No one knows the exact numbers of anorectics, bulimics, or compulsive overeaters, but those who study eating disorders estimate that 90 to 95 percent of people with eating disorders are female—although the incidence among males appears to be increasing, particularly with bulimia and perhaps with compulsive overeating as well.

Even Charles Dickens noticed the prevalence of such disorders among women over a century ago. In a magazine article in 1869, he wrote, "Fasting women and girls have made more noise in the world than fasting men." And as Joan Jacobs Brumberg points out, there were no fasting boys a century ago.

There are many possible explanations, none of which stands completely alone.

THE PHYSIOLOGICAL EXPLANATION. Boys and girls develop quite differently as they reach adolescence. As boys mature, their weight gain shows up mainly as muscle. Girls also develop lean muscle tissue, but most of their normal weight gain becomes fat, which appears especially in the breasts and hips and is related to the maturing of their reproductive systems. While a boy's increased weight is associated with strength and power, weight gain may carry less appealing associations for a young girl living in a thin-is-everything society.

THE SELF-ESTEEM EXPLANATION. As much as the women's movement has accomplished, there remains a difference in how young people assess themselves. Look at sports, for instance. Boys have very concrete ways of self-assessment: batting averages, win-loss records, number of pounds hoisted on a barbell, minutes per mile. For the most part, girls have traditionally participated in activities where judgments are more subjectively made, such as gymnastics or ballet.

If a boy swings a bat and misses three times, he is clearly out. He knows it. He knows he is not hitting well at the moment. Perhaps in his next at-bat, he will do better, he thinks. His young sister on the balance beam may think she has performed very well, with near-perfect balance and grace. But if the judges give her a lower score than she had hoped for or expected, she will likely interpret it more personally than her brother did his strike-out. She may tell herself, *"I'm just not good enough."* This is not to suggest that young people measure their self-worth exclusively through physical activities, but it illustrates the fact that boys have generally grown up with well-marked rulers while girls have less defined measures. And as we will see throughout this book, the state of a young girl's self-esteem is crucial in understanding and treating her eating disorder. One place where she can take a definitive measure of herself is on the bathroom scale: If she is obsessed with her weight, she can watch the hard numbers every day or several times a day.

Some doctors describe this phenomenon as a distorted form of competition. They observe a feeling of superiority on the part of some young women who have eating disorders, particularly anorectics. They began by feeling inferior to others, so in order to become equal, they compete by becoming thinner and thinner. They make themselves become "better" in order to become equal.

THE SEXUAL EXPLANATION. For boys, sexual maturation is generally less threatening than it is for girls. It is often held out as a macho challenge for boys. ("Did you score?" young men ask each other in locker-room lingo.) While a young man is almost expected to participate in at least some wildness, a young woman is expected to keep her legs crossed. Similarly, parents do not blink if their adolescent son demolishes two whole pizzas, but they may become alarmed if their daughter eats more than two slices.

To a timid girl, unsure of herself and of the world she observes, the prospect of becoming a woman may not be comfortable. In fact, it may be absolutely frightening. By refusing food, she can slow down her sexual development. If the anorectic girl restricts her food intake enough to cause considerable weight loss, her menstrual periods will cease and her thin body will look childlike. She will, in effect, freeze-frame her childhood, postponing adolescence and adulthood. Some bulimic adolescents, on the other hand, tend to be promiscuous young women who almost literally throw themselves into sexual situations. But they are nonetheless confused and unsure of their role as young women.

THE FEMINIST EXPLANATION. Although women have only recently begun to be recognized as men's equals, society still represses women, many feminists contend, by strongly urging them to submit to the cult-worship of thinness. The feminist explanation goes like this: Society alienates a woman from her body by treating the body as an object, as something always to improve and to barter for acceptance. Because the fashion, cosmetic, and diet industries exploit a woman's dissatisfaction with her body image, she is constantly doing battle with herself to assert her autonomy.

Writers like Susie Orbach maintain that an anorectic young woman is confused about how much space she is allowed to take up in the world. She is desperately trying to control her need for food and what it represents (love, strength, comfort), while obsessively checking her intake to attain society's ideal of thinness. In other words, she is both conforming to society's demand and rebelling against it at the same time. Through her extreme self-control and food denial, this rationale goes, she is establishing her autonomy and overruling her body, even to the point of starvation.

YOUNG MEN WITH EATING DISORDERS

What about the young men who constitute about five percent of young people with eating disorders? While there are far fewer of them, and far less is known about them, males who develop eating disorders probably have reasons similar to those of their sisters, doctors suggest. Issues of control and autonomy can be genderless. Adolescent males may be responding to a sense of chaos in their young lives by grabbing control of something—food—to gain any measure of control. They may be unhappy with who they are and try to make themselves into someone else, someone "better": thinner, supposedly more attractive, and therefore more acceptable to others. Some young men with eating disorders, particularly bulimia, may be uncertain of their sexual orientation. That is not to say that they are homosexual, but they may be confused about their sexuality.

In a family where a high priority is placed on food or diet —perhaps Dad has high cholesterol, or Mom is after him to eat certain foods and avoid others and Dad resists—a boy may acquire some overzealous attitudes about dieting. His mother may intentionally or unintentionally encourage him to watch his weight, and he may begin to exercise vigorously or run marathons. But it is important to remember that it is normal for a teenage boy to eat a great deal—perhaps 3,500 to 4,000 calories a day.

In such a family, where preoccupation with food exists, a young man with confused feelings about himself and his self-worth may develop an eating disorder. It appears to take the form of bulimia or compulsive overeating more often than anorexia, however. Some bulimic males are high school wrestlers who purge before matches in order to fall into lower weight categories. Runners, gymnasts, swimmers, and jockeys can also be considered "at risk" for eating disorders.

One young man described the course of his eating disorder: "It started with athletics. I felt I had to be the best. I guess it was subconscious at first, anyway. But I was a perfectionist, and I was compulsive about exercise. I was starving myself to be 'fit,' but my body craved food, so I'd eat on weekends and starve during the week. Eventually my weight dropped from 195 to 120—I couldn't keep my mind on anything; I was malnourished; I fell asleep in class; I had no energy to climb stairs. Finally I was hospitalized."

CHAPTER 3

Recognizing Eating Disorders

It is not unusual for teenage girls—and sometimes preteens as young as nine or ten—to go on a diet. Unless they live in another galaxy where magazines, television, and movies do not exist, young girls are intensely weight-conscious. An occasional diet is usually harmless. It may last a week or so and may consist of giving up desserts or having only a cup of low-fat yogurt for lunch. But when does a "diet" become abnormal and unhealthy?

WARNING SIGNS OF ANOREXIA

Parents concerned that a "diet" may be a cover-up for an eating disorder should ask themselves questions like these:

- Has she lost a lot of weight in a short time span?
- Does she set diet goals, and as soon as she achieves them, does she set new, lower-weight goals?
- Has she complained of feeling fat, though she actually looks stick-thin?

- Does she deny being hungry, though she eats very small amounts of food?
- Does she spend a lot of time alone and prefer to eat alone?
- Has she become obsessive about exercise?
- Has she stopped menstruating?
- Does she seem increasingly unhappy or nearly depressed?
- Is she driving herself to excel in schoolwork?

If your child exhibits several of the above behaviors, you need to talk with your pediatrician or family doctor about the possibility that she has anorexia nervosa. The physician can do a medical evaluation and, if the diagnosis is anorexia, can recommend a psychotherapist who is experienced in eating-disorder therapy. The sooner she is examined, the better her chances of a strong recovery.

WARNING SIGNS OF BULIMIA

If your answer to many of the following questions is positive, you should consider the possibility of bulimia and, again, seek medical evaluation and treatment for your child as soon as possible.

- Does she eat large quantities of food at a sitting but does not gain weight?
- Does she disappear into the bathroom right after meals more and more frequently? Have you overheard her vomiting soon after eating?
- Does she appear to diet regularly but still maintains or regains weight?
- Do you think that she eats secretly? Have you found hidden candy wrappers, empty potato-chip bags, and cookie boxes? Have you discovered empty pantry shelves or money missing from your wallet?
- Have you noticed scars on the backs of her hands from forced vomiting? Are her glands swollen?
- Is she abusing alcohol or drugs?
- Does she often seem depressed?

- Have you discovered her bingeing on large amounts of food—often high-calorie, sweet foods? Are these episodes followed by forced vomiting or use of drugs to stimulate vomiting, bowel movements, or urination?

- Does she seem out of control in other areas of her life, in addition to eating? For example, does she seem overly emotional, with wide mood swings? Has she been staying out beyond curfews?

- If she has told you—either directly or indirectly through her behavior—that she is bulimic, do you think that she recognizes her disorder and feels guilty and disgusted after bingeing?

WARNING SIGNS OF COMPULSIVE OVEREATING

Unlike the bulimic, whose weight may fluctuate but usually remains within a fairly normal range, the compulsive overeater is quite obviously overweight because she does not purge after bingeing. If parents are concerned that a child is a compulsive overeater, they may ask themselves:

- Is she bingeing (without purging or fasting) and gaining weight?
- Does she eat only small amounts in public and/or jump from one diet to another—but still gain weight?
- Is she eating secretly?
- Does she seem so embarrassed about her weight that she limits her physical and social activities?
- Has she been showing signs of fatigue?
- Is she making weight the prime focus of her life?
- Has she been depressed or self-deprecating?
- Does she seem aware that episodic bingeing is abnormal, yet fears she cannot stop it voluntarily?
- Is she feeling tormented by her food habits, and does she determine her self-image according to her weight and size? (Like Debby, the compulsive overeater may imagine that life will improve drastically, that she will become a "better person," if she could only lose weight.)

Again, treatment should be sought right away. If her compulsive overeating continues to make her more and more obese, she will face the physiological problems associated with obesity as well as the plummeting of her self-esteem. She needs the help of a physician and a therapist to help her manage both aspects of compulsive overeating.

CAN EATING DISORDERS OVERLAP?

Anorexia and bulimia are similar and dissimilar, and there certainly can be a crossover from anorexia to bulimia, though rarely in the other direction. A "purely" anorectic young woman abstains—she severely restricts her food intake and her weight drops. Some anorectics may adopt bulimic behaviors, such as secretly eating and/or bingeing and purging from time to time. If she does this often enough, her weight may stop dropping and she may even gain a few pounds or maintain a steady but low weight. But if she gains weight, she will more than likely begin rigidly restricting her caloric intake once more. A bulimic may also diet drastically on occasion, but during stressful times, she may resume bingeing and purging.

KEEPING THINGS IN PERSPECTIVE

While the warning signs of eating disorders are of utmost concern, parents also need to understand what is "normal" behavior for adolescents. For many girls in this age range, the onset of puberty and its accompanying weight gain in the hips and breasts spark near-panic. Even though a girl hopes her flat chest will develop breasts, she does not want them to be too large or too noticeable. When new pounds appear on her hips and thighs, she wants—again—some roundness but not too much. At this sensitive age, she needs reassurance that this weight gain is a normal part of maturation and that the additional weight is necessary as her body becomes ready for menstruation and childbearing.

If your daughter starts to diet or talks about dieting, it is not an absolute signal that she is about to develop anorexia. If she occasionally overeats, as we all do from time to time, it is not a sign that she is becoming bulimic or a compulsive over-eater. A parent who cries, "Oh, my God! She must be ano-rectic!" when she eats a tiny meal, or a parent who labels a binge or two "bulimia," is overreacting. But it is not surpris-ing that they would since so much information about eating disorders has appeared in the media in recent years that many people use the terms loosely.

When a preteen or adolescent's eating behavior does change markedly, however, it is important for parents to be calm and reassuring instead of denying her feelings outright —"You don't need to go on a diet."—The focus should *not* be on what she weighs or on how much she eats, but on her feelings. Her feelings need to be acknowledged and vali-dated, not denied or ignored by a parent.

If a previously healthy, seemingly happy child suddenly begins a crash diet as an adolescent, it is helpful to ask her how she is feeling, observe her moods, inquire gently with-out prying, and let her know that you are available to listen whenever she needs to talk. Perhaps she is upset about some-thing in school, a misunderstanding with friends, a boyfriend who has dumped her. Or she may be worried that the pounds she has put on recently will never stop coming, that she will become a blimp.

Whatever her individual reason, she needs empathy from her parents and assurance that some weight gain is normal for her age and that it will not keep wrapping itself around her torso forever. The last thing she needs is a parent flying into a cyclone because the parent fears that her diet is the warning flag of an eating disorder. Eating disorders are far more com-plex, as we will see when we look at them individually in the next few chapters. They are composed of many psychological ingredients beyond a simple desire to shed a few pounds or go on an occasional binge.

Especially during times of stress—such as parental separation, divorce, moving, changing schools, or going away to college—adolescents and young adults occasionally exhibit bulimic binges and purges. Girls in this age group have heard of others who have experimented with vomiting, or laxatives and diuretics, to rid themselves of a big meal or an overly indulgent party weekend. Many young people report that they try such purging once or twice and find it distasteful. For them, it does not become full-blown bulimia. Again, parents need not panic when they learn that their adolescent or young adult has "tried bulimia" if it has only occurred a few times. But parents should be watchful about other things going on in the young person's life: Is she feeling in control of her life? How is she feeling about herself? Does she bounce back after emotional setbacks that are common to all young people? Again, an eating disorder is not solely about food and body size, but also about complex emotions.

But parents will worry over the question, "When does normal become abnormal?" As we have seen, weight-consciousness is not unusual among contemporary teenagers and young adults. But when other behaviors, attitudes, and psychological factors—the warning signs mentioned earlier—are added, the mix can indicate the beginning of an eating disorder, and parents should seek professional help. (More about this in Chapters 8 and 9.)

As you consider the specific aspects of anorexia, bulimia, and compulsive overeating in the following chapters, please keep in mind that these eating disorders can be treated and that their development can be arrested if we diminish the focus on food and weight and redirect that focus to the adolescent's feelings. We will learn to reevaluate our family's attitudes about food and weight, to see food as simply that— as just food. And we will learn that we are not to blame for the eating disorder, but that whatever we have been doing about it probably has not been working successfully. Therefore, we will see that we can change our relationships with a child who does have an eating disorder and begin to foster her autonomy and help her focus on feelings rather than on food.

CHAPTER 4

Anorexia Nervosa

Sheila's Story

When she was younger, her parents and grandparents often called Sheila the perfect child. Around home she always pleased her parents—she was polite, pretty, sunny, and willing to do any chore. Unlike her brother and sister, she kept her room so neat that even her dolls were lined up by height on a shelf. Teachers, Scout leaders, and coaches all praised Sheila. She was never a leader, but she was always a cooperative member of the class, the troop, or the team.

Sheila craved others' approval, so she did whatever was expected of her. Adults showered her with appreciative smiles, and she beamed those smiles right back. Everyone assumed that Sheila was a most happy little girl.

But Sheila's childhood was not without strain. Her family frequently moved because her father's job required periodic relocations. With each new move, Sheila seemed to fit in quickly and quietly with her new classmates and neighborhood children, but she often confided to her mother, "You'll always be my best friend, Mommy, no matter where we move next." Sheila's mother basked in the compliment and embraced Sheila whenever she said that. Sheila was one of her mother's few pure joys. Though she rarely voiced it, her mother resented the family's corporate-gypsy life-style and the stress it put on her to pack up and try to plant new roots in a strange community every few years. Early in her marriage, she had been a trooper, but in recent years her patience had grown thin. She and her husband began to argue about it. Their tension seethed constantly beneath the surface, occasionally erupting into tight-lipped "discussions": there was no loud screaming, but they were never really resolved. Sheila's father maintained that he did not like uprooting the family, either, but that it was necessary to his career and to the family's economic well-being. His wife countered that it hurt the children and her; she was never in one place long enough to make real friends or maintain a satisfying job outside the home. The few times she had found a job she enjoyed, it was time to call the moving company again.

The children were aware of the escalating tension between their parents, but Sheila's brother and sister were so involved with their friends and school activities that they usually walked away from it. Sheila, though, absorbed every word she overheard. Her strong loyalty bound her tightly to her family, but it also confused her. While she loved both her parents, she found herself siding more often with her mother—and this made her feel disloyal toward her father.

As a young girl, Sheila never told her father that she hated all the moving about, but by the time she was ten or eleven, she often complained to her mother about it. And her mother frequently complained to Sheila. By Sheila's twelfth birthday, mother and daughter were confidantes. Sheila was well aware not only of her mother's unhappiness about the family's mobile life-style but also of her mother's frustration with a husband who seemed to put her happiness far down on his list of priorities.

Whenever they moved to a new town, Sheila's mother had signed the children up with a local swim team. She thought it would be an easy way for them to make new friends. Sheila had begun swimming competitively when she was seven, and by the time she was fourteen, she showed considerable talent. Her coach at the time remarked casually, "You've got a perfect swimmer's body, Sheila. Don't gain an ounce." An innocent comment, but it struck a loud, dangerous gong with Sheila. She had never been overweight but perhaps had been a bit chubby when she was younger. Now her body was firm and hard from swimming. Yet she began to think about her body shape and size. Maybe she was getting heavy. Dieting would not hurt. She had noticed other girls in her class who looked a little chunky to her, and she feared becoming like them. She would rather look like the thin models in the jeans ads, she decided.

Without mentioning anything to her family, Sheila began to watch calories scrupulously. She weighed herself every morning and recorded her weight on a chart tucked inside her locked diary. She started working out to an exercise videotape before school, running around the high school track after classes, and bypassing potatoes or rice at dinner. Soon she began cutting down on meat, poultry, and fish. She did this so gradually that her parents did not notice. For breakfast, she grabbed a piece of dry toast as she ran out the door, and she barely ate anything for lunch in the school cafeteria.

In the first three months of her "diet," Sheila dropped ten pounds. Another fifteen pounds the next three months. By the time her parents recognized how truly thin she was—she wore baggy shirts and sweaters not only for warmth but for camouflage—her weight had dropped from 120 to 86 pounds in ten months. And she had stopped menstruating.

When her parents realized the severity of Sheila's weight loss, their routine arguments about the consequences of the family's moving diminished. Instead, they bickered about Sheila and what to do about her strange "dieting" behavior. Whenever they asked her why she ate so little, she simply said she was not hungry—she was "just on a diet like all the other girls."

"Diets are fine, but they should be supervised by a doctor," her parents reasoned to her. "And you're already much too thin to keep dieting."

Sheila politely but adamantly refused to see a physician. Each parent blamed the other for not "controlling" Sheila. Finally, her mother called a pediatrician and described Sheila's thirty-four-pound weight loss in less than a year. The pediatrician said she could not make a diagnosis over the telephone, of course, but that many of Sheila's symptoms and behaviors were similar to those of patients with anorexia nervosa. She insisted that Sheila come in to the office for an examination. A thorough exam would determine whether the weight loss could be attributed to any physiological cause, but if it turned out to be anorexia, the pediatrician warned, the problem would have to be addressed both physically and psychologically.

DIAGNOSING ANOREXIA

Anorexia is replete with paradox, enigma, and contradiction. Before we can comprehend the complex features of anorexia in a particular individual, a clear diagnosis must be made. A doctor who examines a young person for anorexia is guided by four diagnostic criteria set forth in the American Psychiatric Association's *Diagnostic and Statistical Manual of Mental Disorders-III-R* (1987):

WEIGHT LOSS OR FAILURE TO GAIN WEIGHT DURING A PERIOD OF GROWTH. The young person refuses to maintain a weight that is minimal for her age and height; her weight drops 15 percent below the normal body weight for her age and height; or she fails to reach the weight gain expected during a period of growth, leading to a weight that is 85 percent of what is expected.

INTENSE FEAR OF GAINING WEIGHT. Even though she is clearly underweight, she fears becoming fat. Her terror of weight gain is often linked to an obsessive preoccupation with food and body size.

DISTURBED PERCEPTION OF BODY SIZE, WEIGHT, AND SHAPE. She believes that she is fat even when she is emaciated; as Sheila often says, "I feel fat." This disturbance of body image begins at the onset of anorexia, when she may not be overweight at all. In fact, only about one-third of anorectics are mildly overweight before onset.

ABSENCE OF AT LEAST THREE CONSECUTIVE MENSTRUAL CYCLES WHEN THEY WOULD OTHERWISE BE EXPECTED TO OCCUR (AMENORRHEA).

Denial is another strong component of anorexia. It is far from harmless, because denial leads to resistance toward therapy. Like Sheila, most anorectics staunchly deny the seriousness of their self-starvation. When her weight dropped below ninety pounds, Sheila responded to her parents' pleas that she see a physician with, "I'm just fine. I feel great. I won't lose any more."

Many anorectics do not come to professional attention until their weight loss has dropped below 85 percent of their normal or ideal weight. The *DSM-III-R* refers to this 85 percent mark as "an arbitrary but useful guide" in diagnosing anorexia. By the time an anorectic's weight has fallen to that level, the doctor will undoubtedly find several medical symptoms as well.

MEDICAL COMPLICATIONS

The medical complications that accompany anorexia are largely those associated with starvation of any cause. Once an anorectic's weight has dropped so severely, a number of physical signs can present themselves:

- Low or irregular heart rate and low blood pressure. Anorexia can cause a thinning of the left ventricle and diminished size of the heart's chambers, which are associated with lowered blood pressure and decreased cardiac output. If an anorectic also engages in bulimic behavior by vomiting repeatedly, cardiac arrhythmias can occur, which are caused by reduced heart size and by electrolyte imbalances.

- Hypoglycemia, or low blood sugar, following a loss of glycogen and fat stores in the body.

- Hypothermia, or a lowering of body temperature. She is often cold, so she wears layers and layers of clothing. Her inability to maintain body temperature may result from the loss of her body fat.

- Amenorrhea, or cessation of monthly menstrual cycles. In the majority of cases, her periods cease after considerable weight loss, but it is not uncommon for amenorrhea to occur before noticeable weight loss.

- Estrogen deficiency, accompanying amenorrhea, contributes to osteoporosis (decreased bone density, which may place her at risk for fractures). Osteoporosis is commonly associated with the postmenopausal years, but it also occurs in adolescents and young adults with anorexia. This is of particular concern in teens and young adults because their bones should continue mineralizing and growing denser into their twenties or thirties.

- Kidney abnormalities: dehydration and problems in urine concentration, which make her frequently thirsty.

- Gastrointestinal problems, which may include abdominal pain, constipation, and/or a feeling of being bloated. Sometimes an anorectic will overmedicate herself with laxatives to alleviate constipation or to lose weight. The resulting diarrhea aggravates her dehydration and electrolyte abnormalities.

- Lanugo, a downy, babylike hair, covers the body.

- "Chipmunk face"—a minor symptom, caused by the parotid gland's swelling. This makes the earlobes stick out and the cheekbone area look chubby. It is uncertain just why this happens, but it also appears in other types of malnutrition. It complicates the anorectic's view of herself because she looks in the mirror and sees a round face, which may further add to her distorted view of herself as "fat."

EFFECTS ON PHYSICAL GROWTH AND SEXUAL MATURATION

Anorexia can affect physical growth, depending on the age of onset of both anorexia and menstruation. Usually when a girl's anorexia becomes apparent, she is approaching the end of her growth in both height and weight, and she has most likely begun to menstruate. (The mean age for menses in the United States is 12.8 years, while the mean age for onset of anorexia is older, generally 13 or 14.) Relatively little growth in height occurs after a girl starts to menstruate, so most girls with anorexia have reached their full height before their anorexia began. But for the girl whose anorexia appears before she has begun to menstruate, her height potential may be compromised.

Anorexia also affects a girl's sexual maturation. The stages of female sexual maturation are based primarily on changes in breast and pubic hair development. As long as her weight remains diminished, the twelve- or thirteen-year-old girl with anorexia will not have enough critical body fat stored for puberty to progress. In other words, she will continue to be less sexually mature and will look more flat-chested and child-like than her peers.

While it is more rare for boys to develop anorexia, the illness can have more serious consequences to boys' height and sexual development if it begins in early adolescence because boys' development generally occurs later than that of girls. If his anorexia begins at age thirteen or fourteen, for example, he has not yet reached his adult height, and he will be at an earlier stage of puberty than girls the same age.

PSYCHOLOGICAL EFFECTS

Starvation can skew and twist one's psychological functioning dramatically. Just as Sheila at 86 pounds did not physically resemble the Sheila she had been at 120 pounds, she was a very different girl psychologically after her weight loss. The sunny, considerate child became a cranky, stubborn, often arrogant, increasingly demanding teenager. The young girl who had never raised her voice was now arguing heatedly with her parents about the amount of food she ate or did not eat.

Starvation has a tremendous influence on the psyche. Malnutrition causes biochemical changes that affect the anorectic's *thinking, emotions, and behaviors.* For example, as she progressively starves herself, an anorectic is subject to starvation-related irritability and apathy because her body is depleting its fat storehouses, including those in her brain. This can lead to stubbornness, denial, and resistance to therapy.

Early in the course of anorexia, a young woman often describes her state of mind as *euphoric.* It is as if she has timidly stepped into a roller-coaster car, and as the ride gains momentum, she finds her fear erased and supplanted by exhilaration. There is a certain excitement: *"I'm getting control of something here!"* she tells herself as she cuts back more and more on her meals and steps up her exercise regimen.

With the euphoria comes a sense of *control.* A girl like Sheila, who has never openly challenged her parents or any authority figure, suddenly experiences the thrill of rebellion. She feels in control of something—something as basic as what she eats—for the first time in her life.

Some girls say that they feel powerful and in control when their menstrual periods cease. For some, there is a sense of proud accomplishment at reversing this biological process: they have hit the "pause" button to freeze their bodies in girlhood, thereby postponing growing up and the uncertainties of womanhood. The more weight the anorectic loses, the stronger and more powerful she feels.

The early euphoria often leads to a *sense of moral superiority.* In order to feel equal to others, the anorectic girl must make herself "better" than everyone else. In response to her feeling of being "not good enough," she creates an extreme standard. She believes that if she can adhere to this extreme, she can become "good enough." So she establishes a rigid set of food and weight rules for herself, and their very rigidity gives her a sense of security. Sheila, for example, cut her food in tiny pieces and arranged them in a particular pattern, matching the design on her family's plates. She began cooking experimental meals for the family. She served them generous portions and insisted that they finish every morsel. Yet she ate none of her new creations herself. To Sheila, her mighty resistance to the tempting aromas and attractively presented foods was a badge of honor—she could abstain, therefore she was morally superior to those who gave in to their appetites.

But *fear* creeps in as the course of anorexia progresses. As she continues to lose weight, she grows frightened of eating too much. "If I go off my diet for one second, for even one cracker, I'll lose control and pig out," she tells herself. Therefore, she continues to undereat as a kind of insurance policy, just in case she should give in to temptation. In this way, her adherence to starvation is psychologically as well as physiologically reinforced.

At times, an anorectic will binge on a large amount of food —large, in her distorted view. This is simply her body's response to starvation. When she does binge, she may try to whip herself back into shape by vomiting or using laxatives, diet pills, diuretics, or vigorous exercise. Such occasional bulimic behavior does not make her a full-fledged bulimic, however, because she does this rarely, whereas the bulimic binges and purges regularly. (For more about this, see the next chapter.)

Overriding physical sensations is another psychological effect of anorexia. Sheila really was hungry as she watched her family eat—her body was crying from starvation. Yet she reined in her appetite by telling herself, *"I don't need food. I am in control here."* Just as she denied her appetite, she overrode her own sensation of being cold. She would not admit to herself that she felt cold even when she layered jacket over sweater, over sweatshirt, over T-shirt. As she wore gloves in her bedroom when she studied late at night, she told herself, *"I don't feel cold; I feel nothing."*

Obsession with order is yet another psychological effect of anorexia that spills over into many other areas of life beyond food and weight. For instance, not only did Sheila write down her daily weight and caloric intake, but she also recorded the type of exercise and the amount of time she spent doing it every day. And she became compulsive about her schoolwork. Though she had always been a better-than-average student, Sheila threw herself into her studies, taking notes of her notes and reviewing them late into the night, whether or not there was a test the next day. An A-minus was never good enough. Sheila demanded of herself only an A.

Depression, another result of her malnutrition, may eventually replace her early sense of euphoria. The lower her weight falls and the longer anorexia proceeds untreated, the more likely it is that she will become depressed. She clings desperately to the control she has established for herself through the elaborate noneating and exercising rules, and she simultaneously grows increasingly afraid of losing that control. Her most dreadful fear is that if she loses even a thread of the control she has so carefully built into her life, she could lose it all and her life would become chaotic, arbitrary, meaningless. Is it any wonder she begins to feel more and more anxious, depressed, and frightened the longer her anorexia persists? Not only is her body emaciated and fatigued, but her will is constantly doing battle with itself.

PREVALENCE AND PROGNOSIS

How prevalent is anorexia? Several studies have arrived at different figures—from one in eight hundred to as many as one in one hundred girls between the ages of twelve and eighteen may have anorexia nervosa. One reason for the inconclusive nature of these findings may be the different population groups studied. Anorexia appears to occur more frequently in upper-middle-class families; therefore, a broad study of female adolescents in public high schools across the country would likely yield a lower prevalence rate than a study of young women in more affluent suburban high schools, both public and private.

As we saw earlier, anorexia predominates overwhelmingly in females—95 percent of anorectics are female. Usually anorexia appears in early to late adolescence, though some cases occur in preteens and in women in their early thirties.

One of the first questions anxious parents ask when their daughter is diagnosed as anorectic is, "What's the outlook?" Unfortunately, just as prevalence rates are uncertain, the prognosis for anorectics as a group is elusive because no one yet knows the exact number of patients with anorexia, how each has been treated or not treated, how many may have had only a brief episode of anorexia and regained weight without hospitalization or psychotherapy, and how each has fared over time.

Some studies have found that 15 to 25 percent of anorectic patients are chronically impaired by some aspect of their illness.[3] That is, they continue to struggle with anorectic behaviors or medical complications over time, often during stressful periods in their lives.

Mortality rates for anorexia—death from medical complications and suicide—are among the highest recorded for psychiatric disorders.[4] Suicide rates of two to five percent of those with chronic anorexia have been reported. Different follow-up studies suggest that mortality rates for anorexia range from five to 18 percent. There is some indication that mortality rates increase with the length of follow-up of the disorder, with a 10 percent rate for studies that follow patients over several decades.

But these grim statistics should not be overshadowed by the fact that an early and intense combination of medical and psychotherapeutic intervention can improve the outlook.

John Sargent, M.D., senior physician at The Children's Hospital of Philadelphia and director of child and adolescent psychiatric training at the Philadelphia Child Guidance Clinic says, "If you deal with it in the first year, with a girl in her midteens, and you have a good combination of family and individual therapy, with a physician involved, it looks as though four out of five anorectics recover. At least three of five go on to have relatively normal adolescences, though they may have some adjustment problems in college, which is not unusual for that age group.

"If treatment isn't begun until after the first year of symptoms, though, one of two recovers, and [the other] one maintains chronic focus on anorectic symptoms," Dr. Sargent adds. "Over ten years, 10 to 15 percent of those who haven't begun treatment until after a year of symptoms and who maintain chronic anorectic symptoms die of their anorexia."

Findings like these increase the urgency of seeking effective, aggressive treatment as early as possible because anorectic behaviors can become self-reinforcing and self-perpetuating over time. The sooner the detection and treatment, the brighter the prognosis.

"HOW DID HER ANOREXIA START?"

Once families have acknowledged a diagnosis of anorexia, recognized its complications, and grappled with its prognosis, the parents often turn introspective and ask themselves, "How did her anorexia start?"

Anorexia may start suddenly, as an isolated episode of

stringent food restriction, or as a gradual, cumulative process that may last months or years. However any one individual case of anorexia begins, it is important to understand that *anorexia nervosa is a complex condition in which biological and psychological threads are entangled.* It is not a disease whose origin is singular or clearly understood. We cannot blame it on some microscopic bacterium and prescribe a ten-day course of antibiotics, unfortunately.

Nor we can blame it on hormones. In recent years, several studies have looked into the relationship between hormones and anorexia. While there is virtually no evidence that hormonal dysfunction *causes* anorexia, there is agreement that anorectics undergo neuroendocrine changes, including low levels of estrogen, progesterone, gonadotrophin-releasing hormone, follicle-stimulating hormone, and luteinizing hormone. This is a two-way street: Hormones definitely influence behavior and experience—as increasing knowledge about PMS (premenstrual syndrome) has shown, for example —and behavior and experience can also affect neuroendocrine function. As Sheila continued to lose weight, for example, her hormones were disturbed. That dysfunction, in turn, aggravated her anorectic state. While it is generally agreed that both influences are bound intricately together in anorexia, many doctors who treat anorexia—though not all—believe that underlying psychological disturbances cause the physical problems and, as the physical problems then develop, hormonal dysfunction accompanies them.

When a diagnosis of anorexia is made, the physician finds far more than a drastic weight loss and its accompanying physical symptoms. Certain family and personality characteristics also appear to be common among anorectic girls and their families. In order to move toward effective treatment, it is important to understand the young woman within her own family.

FAMILY ENVIRONMENT

Though each young woman is unique, both as an individual and as a member of her particular family, professionals who have studied anorexia have found similar patterns in family backgrounds and interactions. In the 1970s, Dr. Salvador Minuchin and his colleagues Bernice L. Rosman, Ph.D., of the Philadelphia Child Guidance Clinic, and Lester Baker, M.D., of The Children's Hospital of Philadelphia, observed five characteristics that were typical of families of anorectics: enmeshment, overprotection, rigidity, conflict avoidance or irresolution, and the child's involvement in parental conflict.[5]

Before you read on, a few words of caution are warranted. When an anorectic's parents first learn about these five characteristics, many become alarmed and defensive: "That doesn't sound like us! We're not overprotective, rigid, or enmeshed!" The words smack their ears with a harshness that makes them want to turn away. And it is no wonder—they can indeed have the ring of an indictment. As you read this section, please keep in mind that these are characteristics drawn from studies of many, many families; they are generalities, and they may not apply to you. Certainly your child and your family are unique, specific, and individual. But please also keep an open mind. Words like *enmeshed, rigid,* and *overprotective* are not meant to label or blame you for your child's anorexia. Rather, they are descriptions of common threads in families of anorectic children. By looking at these characteristics, you may find insight into your own family's functioning and you may discover some keys that will help you and her in treatment. The goal is to learn new ways of functioning as a family—ways that will blame no one but that will assist you in your daughter's recovery.

Enmeshment

An extreme form of closeness and intensity in family relationships is called *enmeshment.* Boundaries are blurred: who's the parent, and who's the child here? Enmeshed families are so entwined with each other's lives that they finish each other's sentences or answer questions addressed to other family members. Individuality and autonomy are smothered.

Parents may care too much, rather than too little, about their children. They want their children to have the perfect childhood that they did not enjoy themselves, and they tend to be overly involved with their children.

The paradox of enmeshed families is that they are stuck together, yet simultaneously they are terribly alone. They are bound together by loyalty to one another, but they are disconnected personally. And they have a sense that their job is to take care of the other family members, but not to take care of themselves.

In Sheila's family, for example, her mother was so tightly interlocked with Sheila that she chose Sheila's clothes long after Sheila's friends were buying their own. She interrogated Sheila (in a warm, conversational way that Sheila never minded) about Sheila's friends, teachers, and activities. And from the time Sheila was very young, her mother often spoke for Sheila. If a hairdresser asked Sheila how she wanted her hair cut, her mother would reply before Sheila could express her own preference. This became such a pronounced pattern over the years that neither Sheila nor her mother was aware that it had happened.

But when Sheila later began therapy for her anorexia, she began to understand how entwined she and her mother had become. Sheila realized that she had developed a pattern of looking to her mother for cues whenever she was indecisive. From the time Sheila could first speak, the simplest question, such as "How are you today?" would prompt Sheila to look at her mother for a hint. If her mother smiled, Sheila would say, "Fine, thank you." But if Sheila hesitated to answer, her mother would respond for Sheila—in the plural. "We're just fine, thank you." Her mother never asked Sheila how she felt about her performance in a swim meet; rather, she told Sheila how she felt: "You must be thrilled at winning that meet!" If Sheila had been allowed to feel and express her own emotions, she might have said, "No, I wasn't so thrilled. I had to beat my best friend for that trophy, and now I'm scared she won't like me anymore." But her mother did not allow Sheila's feelings to have a chance to breathe before defining them for her. So from a very early age, Sheila often had no clue about what her own feelings truly were.

In enmeshed families, one person may also speak to another through a third person rather than directly. Sheila's father, for instance, always told the children about an impending move to another city through their mother. And when Sheila refused to eat, his indirect way of communicating continued: "Why don't you make her eat? I can't stand to see her wasting away," he often said to his wife rather than to Sheila directly.

Boundaries and roles are fuzzy in enmeshed families because parents do not always act as parents and children as children. The children may act inappropriately parentally toward their parents or siblings, or they may be enlisted by one parent against the other. In Sheila's family, she and her mother crossed boundaries when her mother unburdened her unhappiness on Sheila, and Sheila became her mother's comforting confidante.

The individual gets lost when a family is enmeshed. Autonomy is not fostered but inhibited. Excessive togetherness hampers one's privacy. The boundaries that are supposed to define an individual's autonomy are weak and ineffectual, and family members intrude on one another's emotions. A change in one family member affects the whole family system. Like a stone thrown into a placid pool of water, the ripples go in every direction. When Sheila's dieting behaviors became more and more bizarre, her parents argued increasingly between themselves, and her brother and sister found themselves ricocheting between trying to "make Sheila see some sense," to calming their parents, to wishing to flee the house. As time went on and Sheila's anorexia grew worse, her brother and sister increasingly chose the last option.

Overprotection

There is a tremendous concern for each other in families of anorectics. They genuinely love and care for one another. This concern is not limited only to the anorectic member of the family but is usually evident long before the anorectic symptoms appear. There also is a hypersensitivity to any distress signals—a sense that the world is not a safe place, so we had better band together. A child is not encouraged to take risks outside the family's safety net, so that the development of his or her autonomy and competence is stifled. The children, particularly the anorectic one, respond to parental overprotection and sense that we'd-better-stick-together-to-stay-safe by feeling a grave responsibility for protecting the family. Sheila felt a strong responsibility for protecting her brother and sister whenever they moved to a new neighborhood, for instance. She checked out their new friends and told her parents about anything that went wrong in school if her siblings were concerned.

Rigidity

Change is threatening, scary, difficult, and undesired in these families, so they avoid it whenever possible. Rigid patterns develop to maintain the status quo. A high priority is sometimes placed on being constantly "in control." Slightly weaving out of control, such as yelling even *once* at a child, is considered far out of control; the parent is rendered "violent" in the view of a rigid family.

When a change is thrust upon the family members, such as a relocation to another town for Sheila's family, great difficulty arises. To cope, Sheila's family built a fence of unwritten rules and customs around themselves: the move is necessary for Dad's career, therefore no one is to question it;

as you pack your clothes and toys and books, pack up your emotions, too, and face the world with resignation. Be loyal to the family. Be a good soldier. Follow along.

Rigid families are quite vulnerable to external events—a change of job, school, loss of a relative, separation, and divorce. While they appear from the outside to be untroubled and "normal"—and they believe they really are—they actually deny to themselves that there is any necessity for a change in the way they function. And when a daughter develops anorexia, they see her problem as an isolated, medical one, unconnected to the family as a unit.

Conflict Avoidance

Overprotection and rigidity foster an intolerance for conflict among these families. Bringing any conflict into the open is threatening and, therefore, strongly discouraged. "Keep it under wraps" is the unspoken code. Family harmony is the goal.

There are several ways of doing this. Many families simply deny that any problem exists. Disagreements are defused, sidetracked, detoured, or postponed. Rarely did Sheila tell her parents that she hated to leave her school and the friends she had recently made for a new locale, but the few times she did express some distress, her parents responded with, "It'll be all right; you'll make new friends; you always do." Rather than acknowledging her sadness and fears, they tried to smooth them over and make them go away like an eraser across a chalkboard.

In some families one spouse avoids conflict and the other does not. If the nonavoider tries to discuss a problem, the avoider sidetracks the issue to head off any confrontation; sometimes one will just walk out the door when the other raises a problematic issue. Either way, negotiation cannot begin and the conflict festers, unresolved.

The Child's Involvement in Parental Conflict

Given the above four characteristics, the fifth is almost inevitable. When a young girl has anorexia, it is common that her parents have not been communicating with each other directly. They have been avoiding conflict between themselves and their children for some time. She has been drawn into their conflicts (Sheila as her mother's confidante), and she may either ally with one parent against the other or attempt to be a peacemaker or mediator between them.

As her anorexia develops, her parents join together in protective concern for her. Her symptoms then become something of a regulator of family stability and instability. When she appears to be eating or when her weight stops dropping for a while, there is family harmony. When she refuses to eat, disharmony erupts, often taking the form of one parent blaming the other for not being able to control their daughter. As Dr. Minuchin and his associates point out, the parents occasionally vacillate between concern for their sick child and frustration with her behavior ("Why is she doing this to us and to herself? Why doesn't she try to help herself?"). Her mother and father are so absorbed by parental concerns for her that their marital strife is suppressed or ignored. Her anorectic symptoms have taken over as the main influence on the family functioning.

If you are the parent of an anorectic child, you may be tempted to skip over the next chapter on bulimia. Please don't. While your daughter may now have only the restrictive, self-starving symptoms of anorexia, it is important to know that many anorectics also binge and purge from time to time. When her weight stops falling and begins to rise again toward its preanorectic level, an anorectic may appear to have recovered. But she may also develop some bulimic symptoms. This is partly physiological because it is natural to respond to starvation by bingeing. Additionally, if the underlying psychological causes of her anorexia have not been fully addressed and treated, bulimia may occur as she gets a bit older, particularly when she is under stress. Some studies have indicated that as many as one out of three young people with anorexia have episodes of recurrent bingeing and purging after they regain weight. We hope, therefore, that you will continue reading in order to become informed about bulimia as well.

CHAPTER 5

Bulimia

Jackie's Story

As a little girl, Jackie remembers that she often felt confused. One minute, her parents would tell her how pretty or good she was. The next, they would yell at her for something she thought was insignificant, like the way she had set the table. She could never be certain if she had pleased her parents or failed them. The emotional climate in her home was nothing short of chaotic, swinging from smothering affection to angry criticism. And nothing was ever predictable. Whenever she walked in the door, she didn't know what to expect: Who'd be home? Who'd be in a bad mood? Would supper be ready? Or would she have to fix it?

By the time she reached high school, Jackie was an anxious, slightly overweight girl. When her friends talked about boyfriends, Jackie remained silent. She feared that boys would reject her if she attempted to socialize with them, so she remained isolated. Her isolation, in turn, led them to believe she was snobby, and they made no attempt to include her in parties or to ask her out.

As this unhappy cycle rolled along, Jackie began to think, *"If only I were thinner, they'd like me."* Her weight, which swung between 125 to 135 in high school, was not excessive for a five-foot, three-inch girl, but Jackie became convinced that her body shape resembled a battleship. By her first semester at college, Jackie had begun to binge and vomit regularly.

During her secret binges, Jackie would yank open the freezer door and, with both hands, pull out a half-gallon of ice cream and boxes of frozen dinners. As she tore open the packages and popped the dinners into the microwave oven with one hand, she ate the ice cream with the other. If the microwave was not warming the dinners fast enough for her, she stuffed half-frozen food into her mouth while she searched the refrigerator for leftovers. She consumed this food quickly, with barely a breath between bites. When that was finished, she combed the cupboard shelves for any other foods.

Jackie ate normal meals—quite healthy ones—in front of her family and friends. But after any meal that she thought was too fattening, she simply excused herself with a smile, went to the bathroom, and regurgitated everything. Later that night or the next day, she might binge in her college dorm, but she would vomit that, too, or work out strenuously in the gym.

By the end of her freshman year at college, her bingeing and purging had become so frequent that Jackie was averaging three or four episodes on weekends and two or three during the week. Determined to be a wallflower no longer, she also threw herself into the college party scene. She tried drugs and alcohol and engaged in casual sex with several men, but she developed no lasting or meaningful relationships.

"Inside, I just wasn't happy, even though my roommates thought I was having a ball every weekend," Jackie reflected later. "But I always felt empty emotionally. It was like the binge food would fill me up for a while. Like I could stuff down my unhappiness, smother it with food. But then I worried about the weight, so I'd vomit. And I know it sounds weird, but the vomiting made me feel better, as if it washed away my bad feelings."

DIAGNOSING BULIMIA

Like anorexia, bulimia presents a complex fabric in which physiological and psychological threads are interwoven. Although it is highly secretive, bulimia can be determined by the five diagnostic criteria of the American Psychiatric Association's *DSM-III-R* (1987):

RECURRENT EPISODES OF BINGE EATING; THE RAPID CONSUMPTION OF A LARGE AMOUNT OF FOOD IN A DISCRETE PERIOD OF TIME. A huge quantity of food is consumed, often uncontrollably and rapidly. A bulimic may ingest between 1,000 and 6,000 calories in a single brief binge. Most of the food eaten in a bulimic binge is sweet, high in calories, and of such a texture that it goes down rapidly and smoothly. It is often gobbled with little chewing.

A FEELING OF LACK OF CONTROL OVER EATING BEHAVIOR DURING BINGES. Jackie described her state of mind during a binge this way: "It's like something inside of me takes over and opens that cupboard door. I don't think about what I'm doing. It happens, and it happens so fast. When I'm stuffing myself with all that food, I hardly know what I'm eating—I don't even care what I'm eating. I just know I can't get enough of it." In *Starving for Attention,* Cherry Boone O'Neill described a heartrending evening when she stooped to the floor and binged on scraps in a dog's dish. Others say that they will eat almost anything during a binge, even paper.

PURGING. Purging is the regular engagement in self-induced vomiting, use of laxatives, diuretics, cathartics, or diet pills, strict dieting, fasting, or rigorous exercise to prevent the weight gain that the bulimic fears will result from the binge.

Ironically, laxatives are quite ineffective as a purging device because the food consumed during the binge has begun to be digested in the stomach before the laxative takes effect in the intestines. Enemas and diuretics, also used to reduce a bloated postbinge feeling, are likewise ineffective in reducing caloric intake.

Another and most dangerous method of purging is the use of syrup of ipecac, which brings on vomiting. Families of young children often keep ipecac in the medicine cabinet in case a very young child swallows something harmful. However, if you suspect your adolescent is bulimic, *throw out the ipecac!* A bulimic's repeated and often impulsive use of ipecac can be deadly. It becomes absorbed and stored in the heart, where it poisons the heart tissue, and can eventually kill this most vital muscle.

A MINIMUM AVERAGE OF TWO BINGE-EATING EPISODES A WEEK FOR AT LEAST THREE MONTHS. The frequency of binge-purge episodes is an important diagnostic criterion because an occasional binge does not constitute bulimia. Although public awareness of bulimia has recently increased through newspapers, magazines, and television, some confusion about the disorder still remains. Is a college student who tries vomiting after partying all weekend really a bulimic? Is an adolescent athlete who eats 5,000 calories a day and runs six or eight miles every day to burn off those calories really bulimic?

Before 1980, bulimia was considered to be something of a variation on the theme of anorexia nervosa. When the American Psychiatric Association first classified it as a separate and distinct eating disorder in its 1980 edition of the *Diagnostic and Statistical Manual of Mental Disorders,* the frequency and duration of bulimia were not among the diagnostic criteria.

But the 1987 revision does clarify the issue: a minimum average of two binge-eating episodes a week for at least three months.

Some fashion models, dancers, and athletes vomit from time to time to bring down their weight. Young people in these occupations can be at risk for bulimia, but they would not meet the diagnostic criteria. A young person's "experiment" with vomiting after an occasional binge may resemble an experiment with smoking or trying drugs, but it is not bulimia, either. That is not to say that such experiments are to be overlooked or condoned. If occasional binge-purge episodes continue, they can become an addictive cycle. Young people should be informed about the seriousness of bulimia and its ultimate dangers, both psychological and physical.

PERSISTENT OVERCONCERN WITH BODY SHAPE AND WEIGHT. Bulimics resemble anorectics in their obsession with food, their heightened concern about body weight and size, and their fear of being or becoming fat. Bulimics—particularly those who start out overweight—may lose some weight during the course of their bulimia, but their weight does not usually fall below a minimal normal weight for their height and age. Unlike self-starving anorectics, bulimics do not become increasingly, visibly thinner. Most often, a bulimic's weight fluctuates up and down about 15 percent of normal body weight. There may be cyclic gains and losses over three or four months.

To other people, the bulimic's body size does not appear to be different. Family and friends can easily fail to recognize bulimia because the bingeing and purging are so secretive and because the bulimic's body size is not radically altered, as the anorectic's is. In the support group she joined, Jackie met a woman in her mid-twenties who had kept her bulimia hidden from her family for eight years.

MEDICAL SYMPTOMS AND COMPLICATIONS

Despite the bulimic's concealment, and beneath her apparently healthy appearance, there is no question that bulimia does take a physical toll, which an alert doctor, dentist, family member, athletic coach, or school counselor may detect. During a physical examination, a doctor may detect symptoms resulting from repeated vomiting, including:

- irregular heartbeat
- swollen neck glands
- tears in the esophagus
- gastric ruptures
- hiatal hernias
- infected salivary glands
- scars on the backs of the hands, which result from sticking the hands in the mouth to gag and bring on vomiting.

A dentist may notice other signs, such as:

- damaged tooth enamel, particularly on the inner side of the teeth. If vomiting is frequent, the acidic content of the vomit can erode tooth enamel, and this can result in:
- numerous cavities
- tooth loss
- severe gum disease.

Family and friends may notice other symptoms:

- dizziness
- fainting
- complaints of fatigue, muscle aches, and sore throats.

If bulimia goes untreated, it can lead to far more serious medical complications, which include:

- *Dehydration and electrolyte imbalances.* These are the most serious dangers associated with bulimia because they can lead to cardiac arrhythmias and possible sudden death. Repeated vomiting causes the stomach to lose hydrochloric acid and fluid volume. The body's attempt to compensate for this dehydration disrupts normal kidney functions. The result is an electrolyte imbalance: the loss of essential potassium ions and the retention of sodium ions. Potassium deficiency, or hypokalemia, makes the kidneys unable to concentrate urine and causes muscle fatigue, weakness, numbness, extreme muscle spasms, or epilepsylike seizures. In the severest cases, paralysis and cardiac arrythmias, which can be fatal, may occur.

- *Progressive kidney failure.* This is often found among bulimics who repeatedly vomit. Those who are chronically dehydrated from restricted diets, laxative abuse, and vomiting are at risk for kidney stones.

- *Hypoglycemia, or low blood sugar.* In response to foods high in sugar (which seem to constitute the greatest proportion of bulimics' binges), the pancreas releases an excess of insulin, which plummets blood-sugar levels below normal. This, in turn, often creates a craving for more sweet foods. When frequent bingeing results in hypoglycemia, the symptoms that appear include paleness, sweating, changes in alertness, and/or seizures.

- *Reverse gastrointestinal peristalsis.* Among bulimics who have vomited daily for five or more years, this spontaneous regurgitation has been reported. It is a painful, uncontrollable condition that stimulates even more frequent vomiting. When this occurs, the patient has difficulty keeping any food down for more than a few minutes.[6]

- *Complications of laxative abuse.* For the bulimic who tries to purge with laxatives, their use can quickly become abuse because when two or three laxatives a day become habitual, the body builds up a tolerance for them. Even if a bulimic realizes that laxatives are not effective for losing weight, she may continue to use them because she believes they make her "feel thinner" or her stomach "feels flatter." So instead of taking two or three, she soon takes whole boxes of laxatives. Some bulimics have been known to take as many as two hundred laxatives a day.

  Laxative abuse contributes to the loss of potassium, sodium, and magnesium from the colon. Chronic laxative abuse causes dehydration and excessive sodium in the stool; abdominal pain and a feeling of constipation may result. Excessive use of diuretics also leads to potassium and magnesium loss.

PSYCHOLOGICAL EFFECTS

Bulimia drives emotional life in numerous ways. But first, a somewhat optimistic note: A bulimic does not exhibit the starvation-related irritability and apathy that affect anorectics because her body is not depleting its fat storehouses in the brain, as the emaciated anorectic's is. That is perhaps the reason why a bulimic is usually less denying, less stubborn, and less resistant to therapy than an anorectic. (But bulimics who purge with diet pills may show restlessness, anxiety, irritability, agitation, or sleep disturbances.) Many bulimics acknowledge their disorder—if only to themselves—rather than deny it. Like Jackie, they recognize that they need help.

"Even though I didn't want anyone to know I was vomiting after meals and bingeing at two A.M. in my dorm, *I* knew something was wrong," Jackie said. "I knew I had a food and weight problem that was in my head as much as in my stomach—maybe more, but I used to think I was the only one in the world who did this weird stuff. And I was afraid to tell anyone."

FEELING CONTROLLED BY FOOD. When the binge-purge cycle becomes entrenched and frequent, a bulimic finds that her life revolves around food—what kinds to binge on, when next to binge, and where to do it when no one will be around to witness it. The binge-purge cycle becomes the main organizing event of daily life. It becomes such a central focus, says one former bulimic, that "my life revolved around the neighborhood convenience store. It was open at all hours of the day and night, and it was always stocked with bags of chips and ice cream and brownies." Another has said, "Every morning, I swear to myself that I won't binge out, but all I can think about is food, and that makes the temptation to binge even worse. I know just what it's like for a drug addict who's trying to kick the habit. You can think of nothing else."

Yet in one of the many paradoxes of eating disorders, food is also the enemy. While a bulimic wants to know that food is available and near at hand, she is continuously doing battle with the very food that she craves. Always trying to contain the urge to binge, a bulimic fears not being able to stop eating voluntarily once a binge begins.

FEELING ALONE IN A CROWD. Though a bulimic may appear to be quite outgoing, he or she may feel lonely. Beneath that exterior is a great unhappiness and a strenuous attempt to conceal "the secret" of what a bulimic believes is singularly bizarre behavior. Some truly believe they are the only binge-purgers in the world and therefore consider themselves odd; but for others, their "weird" behaviors make them feel unique, and they enjoy feeling special.

FEMINIST CONFUSION. Unlike an anorectic, who may appear to reject becoming a woman by attaining amenorrhea and a childlike body shape through starvation, a young woman with bulimia may be confused about the contemporary "feminine ideal." She may be a strong feminist, striving for equality, opportunity, and independence. Yet she also wants to be closely involved with others, to please them, and to be accepted by them, so she may become flirtatious, even occasionally promiscuous. Thus the increased opportunities afforded her by feminism cut like a two-edged sword—and leave her feeling scared and confused.

ADDICTIVE TRAITS. After a binge, a bulimic often vomits to decrease the pain of abdominal distention—that "bloated feeling." Vomiting allows her to continue eating, to end the binge, or to relieve her anguish for having stuffed herself. But some bulimics say that the vomiting itself is the desired goal—"I binged so I could vomit"—and they may even induce vomiting after eating a small amount of food in order to reach the "comforting, soothing, numbing feeling" that results from the vomiting.

"It's a way to chill out, to relax," Jackie said. "I feel so calm right after vomiting." For some, the purge seems to take on a purification role, a way of overcoming the self-hatred associated with bingeing. Like smoking or drugs, bulimic behaviors may contain pleasurable and reinforcing elements that operate like an addiction.

LOSING CONTROL. Many bulimics describe themselves as "feeling totally out of control" when they are in the midst of a binge. There is an intractable quality to the binge, as if an outside force takes over. Once the gorging begins, bulimics have compared their sensations to "going to never-never land . . . like being drunk . . . in a stupor . . . nothing else matters but the food I'm gulping."

Some describe the "ecstasy" of abandoning control and surrendering to food during a binge. Unlike an anorectic who tries to impose strict, punitive control on herself and her environment with restrictive eating rituals, a bulimic flounders in an absence of controls. A floodtide of food rolls in, and she can barely tread water while she binges.

MOOD INSTABILITY. A depressed mood is "commonly observed" among bulimics, according to the *DSM-III-R.* Professionals who work with bulimics also notice common traits such as impulsivity and wide mood swings. Bulimics have felt out of control and helpless for a long while, probably long before their bulimic symptoms appeared. These helpless, out-of-control feelings contribute to their low self-esteem, forming a self-perpetuating cycle.

SUBSTANCE ABUSE. Some bulimics are substance abusers, dependent most frequently on sedatives, amphetamines, cocaine, or alcohol. Several studies have shown that as many as 50 percent of bulimic women have serious substance-abuse problems. For those who abuse alcohol, each problem is compounded because the alcohol reinforces the bulimia. She drinks, worries about the calories in the alcohol, gets scared, and tells herself, *"Maybe I shouldn't eat."* But she eats anyway and vomits more of what she ate in response to her drinking. For others, amphetamines or cocaine serve a purging purpose: to suppress hunger for a few days after bingeing.

PREVALENCE AND PROGNOSIS

Because bulimia is so secretive, it is difficult to determine how widespread the disorder is. Research on the incidence of bulimia is recent and ongoing; those studies that do exist vary and often look at narrow population groups. For example, a 1980s study of college freshmen indicated that 4.5 percent of the females and 0.4 percent of the males had a history of bulimia. It appears that the incidence of bulimia is increasing, though how rapidly is also difficult to assess because of the disorder's secretive nature.

While anorexia usually appears at a younger age (eleven to nineteen) than bulimia, bulimia often does not become an established behavior until the girl's later teens or early twenties. And while anorexia is almost exclusively a young person's disorder, bulimia is not necessarily. Some adults are bulimic in their twenties, thirties, and even forties.

The prognosis for bulimics improves if they seek treatment early. The younger the person is and the sooner she finds therapy, the less frightened she is likely to be. But the great problem is that most young bulimics do not get into treatment until they have been involved with the disorder for two to five years. It generally takes about a year for bulimic behavior to develop into an alarming pattern, one that takes on a life of its own. For the first six to twelve months, the behavior is intermittent and under control; they only engage in it when they choose to, so they therefore do not see it as a problem. But after a year it becomes insidiously out of their control, and they recognize its seriousness, even when they conceal it from others.

Once someone has been bulimic for three to five years, it is difficult to overcome without a strong commitment to therapy. The difficulty for a longer-term bulimic lies in the fact that the immediate consequences of bulimia are not all that horrible (as they are for an anorectic, whose starvation is life-threatening). The immediate consequence of another binge-purge is similar to the immediate consequence of "just another" cigarette for someone who is trying to quit smoking. The bulimic says, "I'll do it once and then give it up," but the next time she feels bad, she binges and purges once again.

A firm prognosis is elusive, but some studies indicate that 22 to 25 percent of bulimics "recover" with treatment—that is, they stop having bulimic symptoms and do not have them again. For others, bulimia can go on for years, with and without treatment. But the majority of bulimics have relapses from time to time, particularly during periods of stress or major changes in their lives. (For more detail, please see Chapter 8.)

"How Did Her Bulimia Start?"

That is the agonizing question that many parents ask when they discover that their adolescent has been secretly bingeing and purging for months or even years. Sadly, no simple, single answer is readily available to console or enlighten.

Sometimes bulimia seems to start with a diet. Whether she is overweight or not, a young person wants to shed a few pounds, so she undereats. Then, feeling starved, she eats an amount that would be normal for someone in a starvation state, and she eats it rapidly—but that frightens her, and she wants to undo the damage. She discovers that purging gives her relief. At first, she believes that she can control when and how much she binges and purges. Before long, the binge-purge cycle becomes just that—a cycle that is no longer under her control. And it is usually triggered by stressful situations: a fight with a boyfriend, upcoming exams, a failing grade, starting a new school, the loss of a friendship. But dieting alone is not the "cause" of bulimia.

Several current theories about bulimia's origins point to the notion that bulimia has many determining aspects. Personality, biological factors, sociocultural elements, and family characteristics all come into play.

Personality

Personality traits vary rather widely among bulimics, but two characteristics appear to be consistent: low self-esteem, and a significant degree of mood instability (high anxiety, low frustration tolerance, impulsiveness, depression, wide mood swings). They also share a sense of isolation from other people, feelings of inadequacy, hopelessness, helplessness, loneliness, unworthiness, and despair.

Bulimics seem to have quite high expectations of themselves, yet their low self-esteem contributes to feelings of self-deprecation, shame, and guilt. A painful discrepancy therefore exists between the ideal view they hold of themselves and their actual behavior and feelings.

To understand the personality factors that commonly appear among bulimics, it is helpful to compare and contrast them with those of anorectics. (If you skipped the previous chapter because your child has bulimia rather than anorexia, you may wish to refer back to that chapter at some point.)

As Dr. John Sargent observes, "In the face of life, I think that anorectics say no—no as a way of establishing control because they feel they cannot say yes. Saying yes would get them too much, too much that they feel they can't control.

"But bulimics in the face of life have trouble saying no. They feel they cannot say no because saying no to something makes them lose. Saying no gets them too little. They can't balance their lives. And they say yes too much, until it feels uncomfortable and they have to undo it. They are involved in achievement—social and athletic activities, sexuality, school-work—to such a degree that if they let go of any portion of it, they're scared of losing the whole thing. Then they feel they don't have the capacity to modulate their behavior, either—they've said yes to too much and they feel they have to undo some of what they've said yes to. So the bulimia becomes a stress release, a way of undoing things."

A major difference between an anorectic and a bulimic, Dr. Sargent concludes, is that "anorectics establish connection with others through disconnection, and bulimics establish disconnection through appearing to comply, or being overly compliant. They're trying to be good by being successful, but there is a self-hate associated with the drive that makes them feel that they will only be somebody if they are superstudent, superdaughter, superlover, superathlete, supersocial.

"What is similar about anorectics and bulimics is that they are always paying attention to what other people think of them. The anorectic never believes what anybody thinks of her, so she always imagines that people think worse of her than they do. The bulimic, on the other hand, believes that people think well of her only if she does what the other person wants. So she says yes, and yes, and yes. She doesn't want to disappoint the other person. Another way in which bulimics differ from anorectics is that they probably fluctuate more rapidly from undercontrol to overcontrol, from being all good to all bad."

Biological Possibilities

Whether and how much organic factors contribute to the onset of bulimia is not clear, but recent studies have shown that depression is not uncommon among bulimics *and* that depression is also more common in their families than in families of nonbulimics. The question then arises: Could there be a biological connection, or a genetic predisposition? Research into a possible link between bulimia and depression is still ongoing and controversial. Investigators who have looked intensively at the relationship between mood disorders (also called "affective disorders") and eating disorders have not drawn definitive conclusions with respect to entire populations of anorectics or bulimics. But some individual young bulimics have associated mood problems for which direct psychotherapy, and at times antidepressant medications, can be helpful. Antidepressants will not "cure" bulimia, but some physicians believe that they decrease the tendency to use bulimic behaviors as mood regulators.

Sociocultural Factors

Biological, family, and personality factors alone would not account for bulimia's increased visibility in recent years, largely among young, middle-to-upper-class, white, college-educated women in Western countries, researchers generally agree. What other factor, then, could affect this increase? The answer appears to be a broad sociocultural context in which the feminist movement's ideal converges with contemporary society's strong preference for thin bodies.

The feminist movement has turned the traditional female identity on its head. Young women who reached maturity in the last quarter of the twentieth century grew up, as little girls, witnessing the traditional values of their mothers' and grandmothers' generations: femininity, physical attractiveness, and domesticity. But a quite different ideal has been held out to them as they reach adulthood—independence, self-reliance, and personal and career achievement—as a result of the women's movement. New choices and opportunities for autonomy have presented a glorious challenge for young women who are psychologically strong, a number of researchers believe. But for young women whose self-esteem is low and who are more dependent than independent, the opportunities for those greater personal freedoms can be overwhelming, confusing, and anxiety provoking.

While the confused adolescent or young adult is trying to

sort out just where she wants to "fit" in her role as a woman, she is also bombarded with media hype about thinness: Thin is in, fat is out. In choosing to pursue a career, the young feminist cannot avoid seeing the headlines about recent studies: "Fat execs get thinner paychecks," "Obese girls have less chance of admittance to college than nonobese," "Obese job applicants are less likely to be hired and promoted than slimmer applicants."

Whether she is obese, slightly overweight, or of normal weight, the young woman with ambitions higher than her mother's and grandmother's cannot avoid the thought, *"Maybe if I just lost a little weight, I'd have a better chance at getting what I want."*

Obviously, not all young women growing up in this contemporary cultural environment develop eating disorders. But in a society that emphasizes thinness and achievement, a young woman prone to mood disorders such as depression and impulsivity, whose self-esteem is low, and whose family life is conflicted can certainly be at risk.

Sexual Abuse

In recent years, a number of adult women with bulimia have openly discussed the fact that they were childhood victims of incest and other forms of sexual abuse. Others have said they were rape victims in adolescence or early adulthood. Information linking eating disorders and sexual abuse is extremely incomplete, and statistics vary widely. For some individuals, there is undoubtedly a causal connection between their early sexual victimization and the later development of an eating disorder. But the evidence is inconclusive for the wide population of persons with eating disorders, particularly bulimia; certainly not every bulimic has been sexually abused. Still, many young women who were abused early in life later develop an eating disorder. One described her response: "After my father abused me, I crammed food into my mouth quickly. I felt safe then because food numbed me, calmed me. As I got heavier, the fat was a wall around me so nobody could get in."

FAMILY ENVIRONMENT

Various studies suggest that families of bulimics share similar characteristics: they often appear to be disengaged, conflicted, chaotic, more belittling and appeasing, less trusting and nurturing, and less able to resolve conflict than nonbulimic families because they tend to communicate indirectly and in contradictory styles.

As we forewarned in the preceding chapter on anorexia, these words are harsh on parents' ears. Please keep in mind that they are generalities drawn from studies of many families. You may find some similarities to your family, or you may find that these characteristics do not apply to your family. Please keep in mind that this information is meant to inform, to give you the best current information about bulimia, so that you can understand your daughter or son's eating problems and seek help.

In studying characteristics common among families of bulimics, investigators have observed that these families express greater anger and conflict and exhibit a more indirect pattern of communication than normal control group families. In the families of bulimics, there appears to be less support for each other and less value placed on autonomy and assertiveness, a higher degree of discord between parents, and greater degrees of stress within the family. Some researchers have also noted that the mothers of bulimics tend to be more hostile and depressed than other mothers, and that the fathers tend to be more irritable, impulsive, and more alienated from the bulimic daughter.

In the families of many bulimics, there is little control or structure. In Jackie's family, for instance, the word *chaotic* might well describe her home environment. The chaos that surrounded Jackie gave her a constant feeling of unpredictability: "Will Dad and Mom be fighting when I get home? Will I have to fix supper for myself and my brothers because Mom has been out doing something else?" she would often wonder.

In Jackie's home, meals were served catch-as-catch-can, anytime someone got around to fixing them. Even when she was a very young child, Jackie had no firm bedtime, as her envious friends did. People in her family went to bed whenever they were tired. Someone was usually up at one or two A.M., banging around, while someone else tried to sleep. "I guess by the time I got to junior high and high school," Jackie recalls, "I didn't have much balance in my life. But I was trying to do well in school, in sports, and have friends, and I think I was scared that if I couldn't do everything, my whole life would fall apart."

A bulimic's family often swings in a wide emotional arc. Unlike the anorectic's more rigid family, whose pendulum of behavior and emotion swings in a tight, narrow arc, the bulimic's family has a considerably broader arc, whose time span is shorter as emotions and behaviors swing from side to side. "Oh, we didn't yell and scream at each other all the time or anything like that," Jackie recalls. "But my parents never tried to hide their anger at us kids when we did something wrong, or their anger at each other for stupid little things. But there was always a lot of tension—I never knew what trivial incident or remark might set off an explosion. One minute my parents would be interested in me and what I was doing, and the next it seemed that they couldn't care less. I never could predict if my actions or words would please them, anger them, or put them to sleep."

Addictive and impulsive behaviors also seem to appear more frequently in families of bulimics than in control groups, some researchers and therapists have found. "There is more impulsivity modeled in families of some bulimics— gambling, alcoholism, substance abuse, abusiveness, usually on the part of the man," explains Dr. Sargent.

Obesity is another common denominator that occurs in many families of bulimics. A former bulimic who counseled Jackie says, "I grew up in a family where all the women were obese. My bulimia grew out of my fear of obesity. As a little girl, I told myself that I would never let myself grow up and be so fat."

CHAPTER 6

Compulsive Overeating

Debby's Story

As a little girl, Debby was of average to slightly above-average weight for her height and age. But as she reached adolescence, she began to eat larger-than-normal portions at meals. And with growing purchasing power—thanks to her allowance and baby-sitting earnings—she could buy junk food to snack on between meals, and she did so at every opportunity. By age sixteen, her five-foot, four-inch frame carried 178 pounds.

"I couldn't walk by a store without popping in to buy a candy bar or a bag of chips," she says. "I'd try to take a different route home from the bus stop, but that didn't work. I found myself right back to my old routine within a day. I tried dieting, but I couldn't stick with it. As soon as I'd start a new diet, I found myself so hungry all the time that I'd start eating all over again."

As her weight continued to climb, Debby found herself inventing innovative excuses to get out of gym classes. She bought baggy clothes to conceal her size. She turned down invitations to swim parties, excursions to the beach—any event at which skimpy clothing would be required. The more she withdrew socially, the more she ate at home, alone.

"I was pretty miserable, about school, my family, myself," she remembers. "I used to think everything would be okay if only I could lose weight. If I could be thin, I wouldn't always be hungry, I thought. I'd heard about a girl in my school who was bulimic, and I thought about barfing after I stuffed myself, but it sounded too gross. I couldn't make myself do that, so I just kept eating. And if I didn't have the money to buy some food, I'd sneak it out of my mom's wallet. I just had to eat when I felt bad because I knew the food would make me feel better, for a while at least."

RECOGNIZING COMPULSIVE OVEREATING

Compulsive overeating is not considered a separate eating disorder in the American Psychiatric Association's *DSM-III-R*, but it merits discussion as a form of eating disorder nonetheless. In many ways, compulsive overeating resembles bulimia, but the compulsive overeater tends not to purge. Purging may be occasional, but not as an integral part of a binge-purge cycle. Another difference is that while the bulimic's weight usually fluctuates within a fairly normal range, the compulsive overeater usually continues to gain weight, despite attempts at dieting, well into the above-average range.

Like anorectics and bulimics, the great majority of compulsive overeaters are female; 90 percent is a generally accepted estimate. But more and more men are seeking treatment for compulsive overeating.

BEHAVIORAL SIGNS. Some of the behavioral signs of compulsive overeating include:

- bingeing (eating large quantities of often high-calorie foods)
- bouncing from one diet to another without success
- eating little in public, while weight remains above average
- curtailing social and physical activities because of embarrassment about weight and body size
- increased fatigue and lack of energy.

ATTITUDE SHIFTS. Over time, those who live with compulsive overeaters notice not only their weight gain and increased fatigue but also shifts in the overeaters' attitudes. As in other eating disorders, weight becomes the central focus of life for overeaters. Their feelings about themselves center on their weight and on control of their eating habits. They sometimes talk of feeling "tormented" by their eating habits, and they fantasize that their lives would improve vastly if only they were thin. Any failure—whether social, school- or job-related —is caused, in their view, by their overweight.

When Debby applied for a summer job as a camp counselor and was not hired, she blamed the camp director for being "biased against fat people." She overlooked the fact that she had not applied on time; her application was not submitted until June, when enough counselors had already been hired.

PSYCHOLOGICAL EFFECTS. Like anorexia and bulimia, compulsive overeating is full of paradox. Its messages are simultaneously defiant and compliant. The defiant message is, "I can control my environment by eating; I'm the only one who can control my body, my self. So I'll eat what I want to, when I want to." But at the same time, the compulsive overeater is sending a compliant message: "I'm a mess, totally out of control; I can't take care of myself."

Therapists find that many compulsive overeaters are afraid of dependency. By eating, the compulsive overeater gives herself a false sense of independence. *"I don't need anybody,"* Debby told herself. *"I only need food."* But she is actually very dependent. When she is in greatest need of another person, she feels most out of control. If a friend walks out of her life, for example, her response is to binge. If she has a disagreement with someone close to her, she does not dare to express her anger because she might risk losing that person if she did. Again, her response is to open the cupboard and gorge.

In other words, emotions are experienced as hunger by the overeater. If she feels sad, angry, or afraid, food is her answer. Food solves any problem at hand. Food soothes the ache. Like bulimics, compulsive overeaters use food to cope with emotional distress, disorder, and conflicts. Feeling deprived, empty, and worthless, the overeater fills—and overfills—the emotional void with food.

Once she starts bingeing, she feels out of control, frightened that she cannot voluntarily stop eating. Guilt and shame often follow an uncontrolled eating episode. The compulsive overeater then may try to diet. But this begins a self-defeating cycle: Because she imposes such a rigid diet on herself, the overeater feels deprived, and so she soon swerves off the diet, bemoans the fact that she has failed once more, and begins eating compulsively all over again.

Like a bulimic, she is self-critical and depressed. But her attempts to diet are off the mark because they do not address the psychological needs that led her to overeat in the first place. And like the bulimic, the compulsive overeater recognizes her disorder as abnormal behavior. This acknowledgment is an important first step toward seeking treatment.

WHO IS AT RISK?

Because compulsive overeating is a psychologically based disorder (that is, food is used to meet psychological needs), a young person who has not developed the psychological tools to deal with stress may use food as a way of coping. It also appears that compulsive overeating runs in families, particularly in families where food is equated with feelings: "You're not feeling great? This homemade stew will cheer you up.

You'll feel better," Mama says. Or, "Oh, dear—you fell and skinned your knee? Here, have some cookies and a glass of chocolate milk."

It also can develop in families that overemphasize food: "Eat! Eat! What? You don't appreciate my cooking?" In such a family, no attention is paid to appetite—family members are expected to eat whether they are hungry or not. A compulsive overeater has lost touch with physiological hunger.

Patterns like these usually begin early in a child's life, and gradually, as the child reaches the normal traumas of adolescence, food is always there to soothe, to make her feel better, and even to fill time when she is bored and lonely. Unless it is treated, compulsive overeating can become a chronic problem that lasts a lifetime. Its consequences, in addition to masking psychological problems, can be the same as obesity's: heart problems, diabetes, mobility problems.

Social Attitudes Toward Overeating

Anorexia and bulimia have received such widespread public attention in recent years that both are now taken seriously as psychological disorders. Unfortunately, this has not happened with compulsive overeating. Our contemporary culture generally scorns and jokes about overeaters. Roseanne Barr, who described herself to Sally Jessy Raphael and a national television audience as "a compulsive overeater . . . and obsessive-compulsive," is a comedienne. Would her audience find Roseanne as funny if she were svelte?

Rather than taking compulsive overeating seriously, many people view the overeater as a weak, lazy glutton—someone who lacks willpower, strong character, and self-control. Few look at the deeper dimension, the emotional roots of compulsive overeating. Instead, they suggest that diets, workout centers, spas, fat farms, and fat camps are the solution. But this so-called solution only compounds the problem because it focuses solely on food and weight while overlooking the psychological issues that underlie compulsive overeating.

In an environment where well-meaning family and friends urge the compulsive overeater to try just one more diet program, the overeater herself continues to see her problem with the same blinders as they do. Still focused exclusively on food and weight, she does not consider her eating behavior as all that serious, either. So the cycle continues. By looking at weight as the source of her discomfort, she avoids the inner turmoil and confusion that is causing her to overeat. And by not dealing with those feelings, she avoids further hurt. If she were to lose fifty pounds, where would her protection be? She could no longer blame her size for her distress.

"Sometimes I wonder why I can't just lose weight if I find the right diet," says Debby. "But then I think that maybe I want to be fat because I can blame everything that's wrong in my life on my weight. Like, if somebody doesn't like me, it's because I weigh 178."

EMOTIONAL DISTRESS AND COMPULSIVE OVEREATING

In *Feeding the Hungry Heart,* Geneen Roth writes:

The drive to eat compulsively is not about food. It is about hungers. The hungers of regret and sorrow, of unspoken anger, unrealized dreams; the hungers of your own potential that are waiting to be filled, like a baby bird's mouth. The more you run from them, the more they threaten to overtake you, consume you, so the more you run from them. . . . The more you run, the more frightened you become. Because then you have to deal with the problem you've created along the way: the 10 or 20 or 30 pounds you've gained. Problems that arise from running are only symptoms of the underlying hungers. But they

become realities in themselves that must be dealt with
—so the focus gets transferred from the psychic to the
physical level. Yet when you stop running, you stop
being afraid. It turns out that the fear of hunger is
worse than the hunger itself.[7]

Compulsive overeating, like other eating disorders, does not
exist in a vacuum. People who are satisfied with themselves
and emotionally healthy do not have eating disorders. But for
those in emotional distress, an eating disorder becomes a way
to adapt, to cope, to deal with, or to "solve" the inner turmoil—using food and weight to assuage psychological problems.

Parents and others who love a person with an eating disorder often ask, "Why is she doing this to herself? Why is she
eating so much? It's so self-destructive!" But the compulsive
overeater and the bulimic are not deliberately hurting themselves. This is not a matter of exerting willpower or self-
control. Only when those who are close to the person with an
eating disorder recognize that the disorder is her means of
coping with discomfort and her way of protecting herself, can
they begin to understand that the "self-destruction" is not
intentional; therefore, it is not something she can easily give
up.

With psychological treatment, she can begin to understand
the emotional origins of her disorder and recognize how the
overeating has been her coping mechanism. She will then be
able to turn to food for simple nutrition, not for comfort or
protection. If she chooses to exercise, she will do so for fitness and well-being rather than only to shed pounds. And her
self-esteem will grow as she finds healthier ways of caring for
herself.

CHAPTER 7

Obesity

Robert's Story

As far back as he can remember, Robert has been tormented by nicknames—Tubby, Jumbo, Lard Butt, Tank, Blimp. Even in nursery school, other children noticed his weight. "How'd you get so fat?" a little red-headed girl taunted him on the very first day of school.

Robert cannot recall "getting fat." But for as long as he can remember, he has been much chubbier than other children. And for just as long, he has hated it.

Being teased and left out of playground games that required speed or agility was bad enough when he was in elementary school. But by the time he hit junior high, obesity became a far worse adolescent curse for him than zits, braces, or being the shortest boy in the seventh grade.

Both of Robert's parents were overweight as children and remain so as adults. As they witnessed his agony, they remembered how miserable each of them had been as an obese teenager. They resolved to help their son lose weight. But as they discussed ways of helping Robert, they looked at each other with baffled expressions. "How can we help him? Look at us and the losing battle with the scale we've both been fighting all these years. What can we do for him that we haven't already tried for ourselves?"

DEFINITION AND STATISTICS

Obese is an adjective that is carelessly tossed about, particularly by young people. ("Robert is as obese as a hippo!") But in medical terms, obesity has long been defined as a straightforward matter of weight: A person was considered obese if he or she weighed 20 percent or more above "ideal" weight found in the standardized adult height-weight tables that are calculated by life insurance companies to determine the ideal weights at which people live longest. Your ideal weight, therefore, is the weight at which a large number of insured people, whose sex, height, and age match yours, have the longest lifetimes.

Like the insurance charts for adults, the ideal-weight charts for children compiled by the World Health Organization are based on gender, age, and height. Both adult and child weight tables show averages and simply provide a rough idea of what healthy people weigh. Because healthy individuals tip the scales at different weights (depending on variables such as their build, bone structure, and metabolism), weight tables should serve as guides, not as strict statements of exactly what any one individual should weigh.

While the term *obese* referred to those who are 20 percent or more above their ideal weight, the term *overweight* applied to those who are 10 to 20 percent above their ideal weight. But these categories have recently been modified to extend beyond the numeral on the scale. *Obesity* now takes into account the excessive amount of body fat. That is, fat should account for 20 to 27 percent of body tissue in women and 15 to 22 percent of body tissue in men. Percentage of body fat is usually measured by calipers, which calculate the thickness of skinfolds in as many as eight different parts of the body but most commonly on the underside of the upper arm.

A 1985 National Institutes of Health panel of experts provided guidelines for various categories of excessive weight. This panel determined that a weight that is 20 percent above "ideal" is a health hazard and a weight 40 percent or more above the ideal is "severe" overweight. About 12.4 million American adults (a third of overweight adults in the United States) are in the latter category.

THE INCREASING INCIDENCE OF CHILDHOOD OBESITY

In the not-so-distant past, American families valued chubby children. Extra pounds were thought of as a shield against poverty and even death. Before antibiotics were available, many parents stuffed their children in the belief that they were warding off disease. Although people ate heftier meals in the past, they were also more physically active than we are today. Americans have reduced their physical activity by 75 percent since 1900, according to the surgeon general's 1988 *Report on Nutrition and Health.* Over the same time span, we have increased the amount of fats in our diet by 31 percent.

Today, what we know about the prevalence of childhood obesity is disheartening.

- Nationwide surveys estimate that one in five American children is obese.
- Childhood obesity has grown dramatically in recent years. A study based on data from 1963 to 1980 found that obesity rose 54 percent among six- to eleven-year-olds and 39 percent among twelve- to seventeen-year-olds.
- Childhood obesity often foreshadows adult obesity. The longer children remain obese, the greater their chance of becoming obese adults. Specifically, fewer than 10 percent of obese infants

become obese adults, but the likelihood of becoming an obese adult jumps to 25 percent among obese preschoolers, 40 percent of obese seven-year-olds, and 75 percent of obese teenagers.

• Though genetics are not the sole cause or determinant of a child's weight, obesity does tend to run in families. If one parent is obese, a child has a 40 percent chance of becoming obese. If both parents are obese, the risk rises to 70 or 80 percent.

Anyone who has picked up a newspaper or magazine in recent years knows that more and more American children are too heavy and physically unfit. Headlines have pronounced an "epidemic" of childhood obesity. Readers might well assume that we are raising a generation of soft, lumpy couch potatoes with excellent eye-hand coordination—thanks to video games and remote-control channel switching—but who cannot do a single pushup or run a quarter-mile lap.

Certainly there is some evidence to support this image. The Harvard School of Public Health and Tufts New England Medical Center have looked at national data and concluded that the more television that overweight youngsters watch, the less likely they are to lose weight. This is not surprising: for every hour of sitting and staring at television each day, a child's chance of becoming fat increases from 1.3 to 2 percent, according to different studies.

The reasoning seems clear. Television not only requires physical inactivity, but its program content and advertisements also promote eating . . . and eating . . . and more eating. Sometimes it is subtle; most of the time it is blatant. Several researchers have found that the food references that saturate television in both overt and subliminal messages usually hype nonnutritive foods—foods with plenty of calories but little protein, vitamins, or minerals. One such study monitored a week of the ten most popular programs and found that 85 percent of the foods mentioned were for beverages and sweets. Another found that 72 percent of food eaten on prime-time shows were between-meal snacks (less than 10 percent of which were fruits or vegetables) and that food references pop onto the screen five times every half-hour on average—not including commercials. Considering that the average American household watches television seven hours a day, that's a lot of hinting to raid the refrigerator.

This was certainly true in Robert's family. Once they became aware of their pattern, they began counting how often one of them would rise from the sofa during a commercial and go to the kitchen for another cookie, piece of pie, some nuts, chips, or a can of soda. As they began noticing the frequency, they were astounded to learn that they averaged three snacks during every hour of television viewing.

MEDICAL COMPLICATIONS

Excessive weight places an estimated four million American children, aged six to eleven, at risk for serious health problems—illustrating that the medical consequences of childhood obesity do not hibernate until adulthood.

Obesity puts a child at greater risk than his normal-weight peers for a number of physiological concerns, including:

- *Bone and joint problems.* The child's developing skeleton, particularly the spine or long limb bones, can be deformed by excess weight, causing knock knees or flat feet. As an obese young person gets older, he or she is also more prone to osteoarthritis, a degenerative disease of the joints, particularly those that bear weight.
- Increased susceptibility to *respiratory problems.*
- *Metabolic disorders* such as reduced glucose tolerance, as in diabetes. Childhood obesity is a major player in the development of diabetes, particularly if obesity continues into the adult years. Some 66 percent of people whose diabetes first appeared in adulthood are or were obese.
- *Hyperlipidemia.* An excess of blood lipids, including cholesterol, which is a significant risk factor in coronary heart disease.

- *Elevated blood pressure (hypertension)* may appear in obese children, sometimes before they reach their teens. Although very few of these youngsters suffer overt heart disease in childhood or adolescence, they certainly become prime candidates for it if they remain obese into adulthood. With notably higher levels of cholesterol, glucose, and triglycerides than people of average weight, the obese child who becomes an obese adult is in greater danger for a heart attack or stroke.

If an obese child becomes an obese adult, the risk of cancer also increases. An American Cancer Society study of 750,000 people revealed that people younger than sixty, who weighed 40 percent or more above average, had a death rate more than double that of average-weight people. Excessive weight in adults has also been associated with complications during surgery and pregnancy, with gout, and with liver and gall-bladder problems.

Psychological Effects

Unlike anorexia and bulimia, obesity is not officially defined as an eating disorder in a psychological sense. No "diagnostic criteria"—beyond the scale and calipers—exist for obesity, as they do for anorexia and bulimia. Yet many physicians recognize, as do parents and children, that an obese child bears considerable psychological pain.

The emotional ramifications of childhood obesity are as significant as its medical risks. If your child is considerably overweight, you know how much emotional pain he or she endures every day. The myth that fat and happy go hand in hand may apply to plump, jolly old Saint Nick, but not to the obese child subjected to teasing, prejudice, and worse by peers and, unfortunately, by adults.

Studies have found, for example, that overweight teenagers with the same academic records as their slimmer classmates have lower college admission rates. Some researchers conclude from these data that high school teachers and counselors who send letters of recommendation to colleges may unintentionally write less glowing letters for heavier students. Other studies have shown a similar bias against overweight people in employment hiring and promotion.

Although our society has recently come to understand anorexia and bulimia as psychological disorders, we still have a distance to go to erase the stigma of obesity. Many people look upon obesity as a sign of moral weakness. Thin or average-weight people frequently judge overweight people as having character flaws—"They have no willpower!" But this cultural bias only compounds an obese person's problems. For a child, probably even more than for an adult, such negative moral judgments contribute to and reinforce his sense of hopelessness and poor self-image.

It seems too obvious to state, but obese children feel painfully inferior in a culture that highly values slim and trim. They often avoid games and activities because their size, slower mobility, or poorer coordination makes these experiences difficult, frustrating, and embarrassing for them.

Simply shopping for clothes that fit well becomes a nightmare. Not only does he face the awkward practical problem of finding garments that fit properly, but the child also feels on public display. Standing before a strange salesperson and a three-sided mirror, amid staring other shoppers, hardly boosts his self-esteem.

In adolescence, when forging an identity is life's main agenda, obese teenagers are even more vulnerable to feeling inferior to their peers. They see themselves as failures. Their self-confidence plummets. They focus on their size and often fantasize that the quality of their lives would improve if they lost weight.

Many seriously overweight children do not tolerate frustration easily and find it difficult to delay gratification—all of which can contribute to eating more. If he feels emotionally empty, food "fills him up" in both physical and psychological ways. Food is comfort. Food soothes. Food makes him feel good—for a while. For many obese teenagers, the sad results are isolation and depression. Instead of joining classmates and friends in social or physical activities, they stay home alone. And eat. And watch TV or sprawl across the bed and close off the rest of the world with headphones. Their lives remain passive, sedentary, and food centered.

THE ORIGINS OF OBESITY

As professionals have become more aware of the consequences of childhood obesity, both physiological and psychological, the focus of much early-obesity research has turned to its origin. No individual child's obesity can be attributed to any single cause. Each child's weight gain reflects numerous behavioral, physical, familial, cultural, and socio-economic factors. But among those who look at obesity in the general population, there are several schools of thought about its causes.

Some believe that fat children become fat because they have underlying psychological problems. Others hold that the reverse is true: that a society so dedicated to thinness belittles fat children and isolates them from the mainstream, thereby causing them to convince themselves that they indeed fit society's stereotypes as "lazy" and "without any self-control or willpower"; in other words, they develop psychological problems as a result of being fat.

It is really a chicken-before-the-egg question. Whether emotional problems precipitate obesity, or obesity—whatever its origin—brings about emotional distress, there is little question that the two factors are tightly entwined. But just how much that psychological distress affects the child's actual weight is unknown.

Still other researchers look to the nature-versus-nurture window on childhood obesity. Does the answer lie with genetics or with environment? Or is it a blend of both?

When we look at a child's brown eyes, we know that at

least one parent has brown eyes. That's plain genetics. When we look at a child who is frightened, withdrawn, and bears bruises and broken bones, we know that an abusive environment has caused his physical and psychic pain. But when we look for the origins of a child's obesity, the lines are not always so straightforward. Many obese parents have obese children. Some have average-weight children. Some average-weight parents have obese children. Is there any logic here?

Children may become obese in any number of ways. One avenue to obesity is certainly heredity. Some years ago, one of the country's leading investigators of weight gain and loss, Dr. Albert J. Stunkard of the University of Pennsylvania Medical School, went to Denmark to study the question of heredity's influence on weight. He chose Denmark because its child-adoption register is well known for its detailed completeness. Dr. Stunkard looked at the adult weights of people who were adopted as children and compared their adult weights with those of both their biological parents and their adoptive parents. He found practically no relation between the weights of the adoptees and the adoptive parents who raised them, but he did discover a strong correlation between the weights of the biological parents and the adult adoptees.

In a separate investigation, Dr. Stunkard compared sets of identical twins (who have identical genes) with sets of nonidentical twins (who have fewer of the same genes). He discovered that the identical twins were twice as likely to weigh the same as the nonidentical twins. This would strongly indicate that something genetic influences a child's weight. But it does not prove that weight is determined purely by one's genetics or biological makeup. Behavioral factors—eating habits and emotions—as well as cultural, familial, and psychological influences also come into play.

As Dr. Robert I. Berkowitz, Director of the Adolescent Weight Management Study at the Philadelphia Child Guidance Clinic, explains, "A hundred years ago we had nowhere near the incidence of obesity that we have today. Genes don't change in a hundred years. Genes take hundreds and hundreds of years to change. So how would we explain the fact that obesity rates have more than doubled in the last hundred years?"

Dr. Berkowitz concludes from various studies that "there are genetic components that may relate to one's metabolic rate, but it's not like brown eyes/blue eyes genetics. It's more a genetic vulnerability to a specific environment. It may be that when you have a genetic vulnerability and you're placed in a high-fat, low-demand-for-physical-activity environment, you have the combination to develop obesity.

"Would you be obese if you lived in an environment where there were no junk foods, very few high-fat foods, and less variation in the diet, and where most people didn't have automobiles, televisions, washing machines, dishwashers, and elevators?" Dr. Berkowitz asks. "In mainland China—the culture I've just described—most people are walking or riding bicycles. There's very little obesity. I'm sure the genes are there, because as you see the Asian population moving toward Westernization, you see a greater incidence of obesity. Is that a genetic change? No—it's an environmental change.

"I don't think we have to worry if it's genetic or environmental—it's both, from my point of view," Dr. Berkowitz says. "The gene [for obesity] may be there, and we can't change the genetic structure at this point. But we can alter the environment, especially from a prevention point of view, toward good weight management: a lower-fat diet, more fiber in the diet, exercise—and I'm not talking about climbing mountains, but walking on a regular basis, generally more physical activity."

METABOLISM AND GROWTH PATTERNS

Physicians who work closely with obese children and their families stress that every child is different physiologically. Just like adults, one child's metabolism is not the same as another's. One individual's body may be more efficient at using its food energy than another's. Sally and Tess, for instance, are both sixteen years old, five feet, two inches tall, and weigh 130 pounds. This places them in the overweight, rather than the obese, category. The ideal weight for girls this age and height is 114 pounds. Sally maintains her 130 pounds on 2,400 calories a day, but if she cuts down to 1,800 calories a day, she can lose a few pounds at a moderate rate. Tess maintains her 130 pounds on 1,200 calories a day. But if Tess wants to lose weight, she has to cut her calories to 800 daily. She is fighting quite a different battle from Sally.

Just as every girl's body handles calories differently, not all calories are alike. The body can store calories that come from fat, via butter or ice cream for example, with very little effort. But calories from carbohydrates and proteins must be converted to fat in order to be stored, and that conversion demands energy. In other words, the body burns some calories to store others.

While it is important to keep in mind each child's uniqueness in terms of individual body shape, bone structure, and metabolism, it is also important to recognize normal growth patterns in overall child development. There are three time periods when the number of fat-storing body cells increases rapidly; once those fat cells are formed, they may grow fatter or slimmer but they do not disappear. The first time period is before birth, the second is during infancy, and the third is early adolescence. Each of these three periods of rapid gain seems to prepare the child for the next developmental stage of growth. The infant's fat cells become more numerous, for example, to store energy that his little body will need as he begins to crawl and stand and walk. The thirteen- or fourteen-year-old boy may look a bit chunky as his fat cells prepare him to shoot up several inches in height and to develop a more muscular body shape as a full-fledged young man.

These three stages reflect typical growth patterns, so spurts of weight gain during these time periods should not cause alarm. There are three different periods in a child's life, however, that appear to be conducive to onset of obesity: late infancy, early childhood (about age six), and mid- to late adolescence (as opposed to early adolescence). Excessive weight gain at these times should be of some concern because it does not signal imminent growth of the skeletal system or other stages of normal physical development.

Another common growth pattern observed in many overweight children appears to be faster-than-average maturation. They tend to be tall for their age; their bone development is more advanced; and girls tend to begin menstruating earlier. Although these signs of advanced growth are not alarming in themselves, they can help predict which children may be vulnerable to excessive weight gain.

TREATMENT OF CHILDHOOD OBESITY

Before discussing positive ways of treating obesity in children and teenagers, it is important to recognize and eliminate common approaches that do *not* work. Perhaps the most obvious "solution" tried by many families is clicking off the TV set, sending children outside to the playgrounds and ballfields, and putting them on diets. But that approach is too simple. As parents and children who have attempted it know, it rarely works. For some families, pushing children outside to play means thrusting them into neighborhoods where drugs and crime threaten their safety. In many families where the children arrive home from school before Mom or Dad returns from work, the television serves as a baby-sitter, keeping youngsters safely at home. Anyone driving through leafy suburban developments during after-school hours sees few children riding bikes or roller-skating on the smooth, deserted sidewalks.

As if getting children to become more physically active were not difficult enough, dieting is no easier. Dieting is challenging for adults because it requires considerable maturity and motivation—qualities that elude most children and adolescents. And most attempts to diet simply do not work. How many times have you yourself tried to lose weight, only to regain it? How many people do you know who have enslaved themselves to a rigid diet but no matter how diligently they try, the pounds reappear sooner or later?

This was true in Robert's family. Whenever his mother read about a new diet in a magazine, she would plan a new diet menu for the week, restock the kitchen with the proper low-calorie ingredients, and try diligently to keep the family on the diet. She would find that after a week, everyone hated it.

"What's tonight's water-and-celery entree, Mom?" Robert would ask. His between-meal snacking would only increase. On the way home from school, he would stop by a vending machine for a candy bar. Or wolf down a bag of chips at a neighbor's house after dinner. As he did so, Robert would feel miserable. He loved sweet or salty tastes, but he hated being fat. He would feel guilty and dejected. *"Maybe I'll never lose weight. Maybe I'll just keep eating and eating and pop like an overinflated balloon,"* he told himself.

Redirecting the Focus

Because simplistic directives like "Eat less and exercise more" and "Unplug the TV and run some laps" turn children off, they are ineffective. A more successful approach to the complex challenges of childhood obesity begins with shifting the focus away from weight loss alone and toward more healthful attitudes about eating and exercising.

When concern about a child's weight becomes the centerpiece in a family's life, everyone's anxiety rises. Parents dig in their heels. Battle lines are drawn, if unintentionally. Parents —and sometimes siblings—view reducing the child's weight as a "project," a mission to accomplish, a war to be won. Every meal becomes a battleground. Such an attitude makes some obese children feel passive, as if they were someone to be "fixed" by outside forces or a victim who does not deserve blame and therefore need not assume any responsibility. Other obese children and teens become defensive, resistant, and highly sensitive to everything food- or weight-related.

In Chapter 4, about anorexia, it was noted that a family often focuses on the child's anorectic behaviors to the exclusion of other unresolved conflicts within the family. This can also happen in families where the obese child becomes a high-priority "project" to be worked on. When the family focuses tightly on reducing the child's weight, his obesity may diffuse other underlying family conflicts. The family's status quo is maintained as those conflicts remain camouflaged. But a catch-22 situation exists here. If the child is anxious, frustrated, angry, or lonely because of unresolved family problems, his obesity is only compounded. He may well use food as a retreat from or a "solution" to his disquieting feelings. Family therapy is recommended to help resolve family issues that relate directly and indirectly to the child's obesity.

To redirect the family's focus from the child's weight problem, it is helpful to assess the food attitudes and behaviors within the family. You could ask yourself questions like these:

- How important is food in our home? Is it used for nonnutritive purposes, such as to reward? to bribe? to soothe and comfort? to appease boredom? to accompany television viewing?
- Do we have "treat" foods for special occasions? Is dessert a reward for finishing the main course?
- What are our mealtimes like—chaotic? calm? Do we eat breakfast on the run? Do we have a relaxed, conversational dinner?
- Do I insist that all members of the family sit down together and eat at a regular time? Do I require that the children eat everything on their plates? Do I offer choices? Who decides the size of the portions—parent or child?

There are no right or wrong answers to these questions. Their purpose is simply to help you take a fresh look at the role that food plays in your family's daily life. Food's role is often taken for granted, but you can alter it as you develop a plan for treating your child's weight problem.

A Multifaceted Approach

Professionals who have successfully treated obese children and teenagers offer no single treatment prescription. Most agree that a multifaceted approach is best—one that incorporates diet, exercise, and behavioral approaches. In cases of extreme obesity, some physicians may also recommend aggressive treatments such as modified fasting over several weeks. The facets that you and your child choose need to match comfortably your child's temperament, needs, and style. Going to a "fat camp" for the summer may work for one child, for example, while another child might hate and resist it.

FIRST A PHYSICAL. Any multifaceted approach should begin with an examination by a physician. This assessment would include the child's growth history, anthropometric data such as height, weight, upper arm circumference, and triceps fatfold, as well as blood pressure and family medical history. Also helpful in the initial exam are a fitness test to assess the child's endurance, strength, flexibility, and cardiovascular fitness, and an interview with the child to gauge self-image and motivation.

SETTING GOALS. After the initial medical exam, goals for weight loss and increased physical activity can be set. The child's input is important at this crucial juncture. If the goal is set by the physician or parent alone, the child will feel passive or resentful, and his motivation can falter.

A crucial first step in helping obese youngsters to control their weight is for everyone involved to recognize that children and parents share the same goal—to lose weight, shape up, and feel better about themselves. But parents and children do not always take the same route toward that goal.

The scores of overweight youngsters whom he has treated, Dr. Berkowitz says, "have always said they want to lose weight, but it's the method, the style of the parents, that's turned them off, not the goal. If parents are nagging or averse or pejorative and put the child down, then the child is going to resist. Parents need to be supportive and to understand that there are going to be little lapses on the way to treatment success."

Frequently, the child's or parent's initial weight-loss goals are unrealistically grand. A child may declare, "I won't eat any junk food for three weeks," or, "I want to lose twenty-five pounds by next month's school dance." Specific goals both for weight loss and for improved eating behaviors should be quite conservative in order to be realistic and attainable. Long-term success depends on taking slow, steady steps. If parents and children both recognize at the outset that some plateaus and slips are normal, the occasional binge or diet downfall will not be treated as an international crisis.

When dieters backslide and put on a few pounds instead of shedding them, they frequently throw up their hands, saying, "I knew I couldn't stay on this diet!" Then they give it up entirely. But successful dieters—those who lose weight and keep it off—have found that slow, gradual improvement results from a moderate, long-range commitment, often of a year's duration.

HELPING THE CHILD TAKE CONTROL. A goal for all children—normal-weight and overweight alike—should be to learn to take control of their own eating behaviors. Though we parents can pull back to give children more autonomy, we need not relinquish all responsibility. Parents are still the gatekeepers —we determine what food is purchased and brought into our homes. We can make it easier for children if we do not stock the cupboards with junk foods, if we offer apples and carrot sticks instead of chips and cookies, and if we try to provide regular mealtimes instead of erratic ones. Many professionals who work with overweight children agree that irregular, catch-as-catch-can mealtimes make it difficult for a child to maintain a healthy balance between hunger and satisfaction, just as easy access to snack foods both inside and outside the home fosters excessive eating.

The late Hilde Bruch, M.D., professor of psychiatry at Baylor College of Medicine and a pioneer in the understanding of eating disorders, noted that many parents of both anorexic and very obese children can be domineering and solicitous, tendencies that hinder their children from developing the ability to regulate the amount of food they eat. From a very early age, a child of such a parent learns to ignore or override his internal cues if the parent constantly regulates feeding.

When our bodies sense that we have eaten enough, we experience a feeling called *satiety* that leads us to put down the fork and push the plate away. If a one-year-old stops eating and begins to play with his food, a parent can assume that he has had enough to eat. A general pediatric guideline is that a baby's weight triples in the first year of life. Then the rate of weight gain tapers off for a while. When a one-year-old's appetite seems to diminish, it is a normal response to the fact that his growth rate is starting to slow after his first year. But a parent who does not realize this and picks up the spoon, jams it into the child's mouth, and insists that he finish eating all his mashed potatoes—instead of fingerpainting with them—becomes an external satiety regulator. If this pattern occurs consistently, the child will not learn to interpret and trust his own internal signals.

In Hilde Bruch's observations, many anorectic and obese young people learned over the years that the ability to control or regulate their food intake was displaced somewhere outside of themselves and that that was one cause of their under- or overeating. They simply did not recognize or trust their own body's messages telling them if they were hungry or full. Or as Robert sometimes wondered, *"Am I hungry? Am I full? I don't really know."* If food was available, he would eat it anyway.

THE NUTRITIONIST'S ROLE. Another important component in the early stages of weight control is consultation with a nutritionist who can help a family look at its eating patterns and find ways to modify them—not only for the overweight child but for the whole household. A nutritionist can take food records from the entire family that show both individual and family eating patterns and can establish baselines from which to make changes. The nutritionist can provide education and information to make meals attractive, delicious, healthy, and satisfying.

This may sound like a recipe for pie-in-the-sky, but diets that are solely restrictive, bland, and unappealing rarely succeed. A dieter who constantly tries not to "give in" to food usually feels deprived, restricted, or even punished. A feeling of deprivation can lead to food-seeking. The dieter may react by bingeing or by eating impulsively. She may become preoccupied with food. Instead of regulating her intake according to her internal cues for hunger or satiety, she focuses on external regulation: a number on the scale, a daily calorie count, prejudices about which foods are "good" or "bad." Various studies have shown that dieters so preoccupied with food tend to overeat. That preoccupation can kick off a nasty cycle: lean body tissue is lost, then regained as fat; metabolic rates slow; and there is less physical activity. So these dieters gain weight instead of lose it.

But weight-management plans do not have to be solely restrictive. A nutritionist can help to plan satisfying meals that provide energy to keep hunger at bay. Such meals include a balance of protein, fat, and carbohydrates in a bulky, chewy variety and are low in calories, yet delicious. When children begin to eat in this way, they can also learn to rely on internal cues of hunger. They take control and their self-esteem and motivation increase.

CHECKPOINTS ALONG THE WAY. As your family makes changes in its diet and eating patterns, there can be various checkpoints to stop and ask, "How are we doing?" The question should not be, "How many pounds has Robert lost?" but, "What changes are we making to promote a healthier eating environment for Robert and for all of us?" Progress in weight management should not be judged so much by a daily weigh-in as by the overall changes that have been incorporated into the family's daily living patterns. More concrete questions to ask at these checkpoints include:

- Are we decreasing our nonnutritive uses of food? Is there less "recreational" eating? Less munching in front of the television?
- Are we eating fewer high-fat, processed foods? More fruits and vegetables? Fewer sweet, fatty desserts?
- Are we enjoying more regular and relaxed mealtimes? Do we eat more slowly and have more conversations at the table?
- Are we encouraging the child when he loses a few pounds, or do we criticize and nag when he doesn't?

PHYSICAL ACTIVITY. Just as you can stop occasionally to reassess family eating patterns, you can also ask yourself some questions about the family's physical activity:

- What kind of a role model am I? Do I spend a lot of time sitting as I read, watch TV or spectator sports? How often do I jog, ride a bike, or swim?
- When was the last time our family took a walk together? A hike in the woods? How often do we swim or play tennis together?
- How much time do I spend driving my children to piano lessons, ballet classes, shopping malls, and friends' homes? Could they walk or ride their bikes instead?

Increased physical activity alone will not guarantee weight loss, but it is an important component of any weight-management program. Not only will exercise burn some calories, but increased fitness can give a child energy and self-confidence and a greater sense of self-esteem. Just as weight-loss goals must be gradual and realistic if they are to be attained, so too must goals for increased exercise be gradual and realistic. Do not expect an obese child to become a marathon runner in two weeks. Most overweight children and teenagers have long avoided sports and other forms of physical activity because they feel awkward or embarrassed. Demanding that they join the soccer team may not be reasonable when everyone else on the team is a much swifter and more agile runner. Perhaps lifting weights, cycling, or signing up with the wrestling team would be more appropriate, as Robert's family found.

Overweight children, as well as adults, should consult a physician to plan a safe, healthy exercise program. For weight management to be effective, it needs to begin with activity levels where children and teenagers are comfortable: fast walking around the block, dancing to music in the privacy of their bedrooms, shoveling snow—even walking up and down stairs. For a 175-pound person, ten minutes of continuous walking upstairs burns 202 calories and ten minutes of walking downstairs burns 78 calories—compared with 14 calories expended in ten minutes of sleeping or watching TV. While hanging out at the shopping mall, overweight youths might benefit by avoiding the escalators and walking up and down the stairs!

Exercise does burn calories, but not many when compared with the calories that can be consumed in one fast-food meal. If the teenager who walks vigorously up and down the mall stairs stops off for a 600-calorie bacon double cheeseburger (which is 53 percent fat, or the equivalent of seven pats of butter), he quickly wipes out the benefits of stair-walking.

Even though this may seem discouraging, exercise does

have other long-term benefits. It helps to maintain muscle tissue when one is on a weight-loss program. When dieting and exercise are combined, there is a greater proportion of fat lost and less muscle than when dieting is the sole ingredient in a weight-loss regimen.

Exercise also contributes to reducing high blood pressure and cholesterol levels and helps improve heart conditions and diabetes, even when little or no weight is lost. Finally, several studies have shown that people who exercise while dieting are more likely to keep the pounds off than those who simply reduce their caloric intake without exercising.

KEEPING THE WEIGHT OFF. When obese children gradually begin to lose weight through a combination of changes in their eating behaviors, exercise, and attitudes, it may seem that they are on the road to "recovery." But parents should be aware that keeping weight off may be even more difficult than losing it in the first place. Even the most dedicated dieter is tempted daily by the delicious, rich foods pictured on television, in magazine ads, and on billboards. Food is easily accessible to most people in our culture—how far away is the nearest fast-food restaurant or corner convenience store from you? At the same time, psychological factors also threaten the dieter's resolve. When a stressful situation arises and makes the dieter anxious, the old habit of heading for the refrigerator reappears.

As researchers have charted dieters' tendency to regain weight after losing it, a recent theory about it has emerged. The "set point" theory suggests that one's body has something of an internal weight regulator, analogous to a thermostat, that repeatedly brings one's weight back to a set point or level. If your weight drops too far below your set point, your body fights back in order to pull you up again to your set point.

Several studies have found that repeated weight gain and loss—called "yoyo dieting"—leads to even greater difficulty in losing weight and keeping it off. A Harvard research project, for example, looked at records of 140 dieters who lost weight, regained it, then tried again to lose it. In the first week of their first diet, they lost an average of 2.3 pounds, but only 1.3 pounds in the first week of their second diet. Researchers conclude that the body learns from repeated yoyo dieting to live on less food because the body views a diet as famine and therefore works to protect itself by using and storing calories more efficiently. An investigation at the University of Pennsylvania found that the pounds yoyo dieters shed as muscle are regained as fat; and that fat tends to be stored in the abdomen, which increases the risk of heart disease and diabetes.

Weight-control experts reach several conclusions from this discouraging evidence about yoyo dieting:

- The repeated ups and downs in a dieter's weight predict little long-range success in keeping excess weight off.
- If a weight-control program is to be successful, the dieter needs to make a serious commitment to changing eating and exercising habits permanently. He or she should aim for a gradual, steady weight loss, not an immediate drop in pounds.

WHAT PARENTS CAN DO. Parents of obese children often feel caught between the clichéd rock and a hard place. You watch painfully as your child suffers the burdens of low self-esteem, teasing, and loneliness. You desperately want to help, yet you often feel paralyzed—"If I harp on dieting and exercise, that will make my child feel worse and eat more. But if I don't intervene, she may never lose any weight."

Do you feel that you're being asked to walk a tightrope? To deemphasize food and weight while simultaneously emphasizing healthier eating and exercise habits? Yes, in many ways you are. It *is* a fine balancing act to catch yourself before you blurt out, "I don't think you should eat that, dear," as your child reaches for a second or third helping. You are trying to get off your child's back, to encourage him to make his own food choices even if you may not agree with them. At the same time, you are trying to encourage more physical activity without sounding like a coach blowing a screeching whistle, which would only push an overweight child further into a sedentary corner.

As parents, we face judgment calls hundreds of times a day —when to shut up, when to speak up, what to say to encourage and support rather than to criticize and deflate. We certainly will not always make the right calls. No one can expect to, but we can try to step back every once in a while and recognize that our children want the same for themselves as we do: good physical health and emotional well-being. There is no single, rigid pathway to achieve these goals. There will be many potholes and stumbling blocks, but the journey need not be gloomy. By eating regular meals of healthy, low-fat foods and becoming more physically active, our children can gain self-esteem and enjoy it—even if they do not drop down to an "ideal" weight. If we recognize that each child is unique, with an individual metabolism and shape, we can accept each child for his or her uniqueness. Not every child has to be—or should be—as slim as a blue-jeans model.

PSYCHOLOGICAL HELP. Obesity treatment should take into account the child's feelings about himself. Psychologists who treat obese children note that weight reduction alone does not always resolve the obese child's psychological problems. Unless those are addressed, his weight may ultimately be adversely affected. Although his body has become thinner, he may continue to carry the baggage of poor self-image and lack of confidence. In the mirror of his own mind, he still sees a fat child and hears the taunts Lard Butt or Fatso. Because he has long been fighting the psychological demons of obesity, his social and psychological development may have been delayed, leaving him without the inner resilience to adjust to all the non-weight-related challenges of adolescence. Without those inner resources and without adequate self-esteem, he may again turn to food and put back the lost pounds. It is important, therefore, for parents to be aware of this possibility and to seek psychological counseling if their child appears to need it.

The next two chapters pertain to seeking therapy for anorexia, bulimia, and compulsive overeating. You may find it helpful to read them if you think your obese child could benefit by counseling. Much of the information about selecting and working with a therapist and about the course of therapy can apply to the struggles of an obese youth who is trying to refocus away from food.

CHAPTER 8

Treatment of Eating Disorders

Parents may suspect for some time that their child has an eating disorder, but they cannot truly believe it. If they question the child, she denies having any problem: "No, I didn't vomit last night and the night before that," or "I wasn't the one who finished off the brownies." If confronted with evidence, such as slices of last night's meat wrapped in a napkin and tossed into the trash, she simply ignores her parents, goes to her room, and shuts the door.

In many families, a parent who suspects a disorder sits down with the other parent to discuss it, and the other denies or minimizes the problem, especially if the second parent does not spend as much time with the child and has not noticed odd symptoms or behaviors. "Oh, just let's see what happens," that parent tells the more concerned one.

As parents wait to "see what happens," they only become more worried and the child's condition becomes worse. At this point, some young people send out SOS signals themselves. Jackie's mother began to notice, for example, that the toilet-bowl brush was frequently left out, propped against the bathroom wall, instead of in its usual place in the cabinet under the sink. Leaving the brush in plain sight was Jackie's cry: "Notice what I'm doing—I'm in trouble!"

Despite noticing the outward signs and harboring their own suspicions, many parents find it extremely difficult to seek psychotherapy for personal or family problems. They feel embarrassed or ashamed that they have "failed" to bring up a happy, healthy, well-adjusted child.

In the last twenty-five years, psychotherapy has become more prevalent and accepted, particularly since Congress mandated that each state establish a system of community mental health centers to help the estimated 15 percent of Americans who have mental health problems of one kind or another. Yet despite the increased acceptance and availability of psychotherapy, many people still balk at engaging in it themselves. For whatever reason, psychotherapy still carries a stigma. "Therapy is fine for somebody else, but I don't think it's for us" is a view often expressed by uncomfortable parents.

Some prefer to view their child's eating disorder as strictly a physical problem—"She's just lost too much weight and she's dehydrated," an anorectic's father told his friends. "She needs to be hospitalized until she regains a few pounds, and then she'll be fine."

But most parents know better. The previous chapters have explained that eating disorders are not solely about food and eating. These disorders are manifestations of emotional distress, and their major psychological components cannot be ignored.

Don't Procrastinate

"If parents suspect an eating disorder," advises Dr. Gail B. Slap, Director of the Adolescent Medicine Section at The Children's Hospital of Philadelphia, "they should not wait to see what happens, especially if the adolescent has lost weight. Parents must recognize that adolescents with eating disorders quickly learn to camouflage their behavior. They wear baggier clothes around the house; girls will no longer undress when their mothers are present; they become more reclusive and secretive. The parent who waits for signs of vomiting in the bathroom may miss an adolescent who desperately needs help. Many parents assume that their teenager does not have an eating disorder unless she's vomiting, and that is absolutely untrue. Parents may never see signs of vomiting or laxative or diuretic abuse. So they need to be aware and not be easily dissuaded."

Like Jackie's mother, parents may have read the road signs but ignored the direction in which they were pointing. But when they recognize certain definitive symptoms of an eating disorder, they must face the fact that the problem is not going to evaporate by itself. The time has come to meet it head on.

Taking the First Step

The most important first step is to seek professional treatment —this is indisputable—as soon as possible. Today.

- Call your family doctor or pediatrician.
- Spell out your specific observations of your child's behaviors and attitudes.
- Schedule both a medical examination and a psychological evaluation.

Physical and psychological evaluations are both crucial at the outset. It is helpful to do the medical exam first because the therapist who will do the psychological evaluation needs the medical results in order for the psychological portion to be coherent and complete.

TELLING YOUR CHILD

Once an appointment is scheduled, it is important for both parents to agree on how and when to approach the child with the fact that she must see a doctor. Parents need to be consistent and united in that approach. This is equally important if the parents are separated or divorced.

"I would not recommend approaching her at the dinner table," suggests Dr. Slap. "That is like approaching the teenager who comes in drunk after a Saturday night party, when parents' tempers are at the shortest fuse. Nobody can deal with the situation rationally at that point, when there's so much emotion invested. The better thing to do is not to talk about it at that moment, but to sit down at a quiet, private moment when siblings aren't around, with the parents united, and say 'We have a problem here,' and remove it from the food issue. Remove it from the 'You're not eating anything!' of the table scene."

Even in a calm setting and time, parents should steel themselves to be firm. Dr. Slap compares the approach parents should take when facing an eating disorder to the approach they would take upon discovering their child was using drugs. "They are hidden behaviors," Dr. Slap explains, "behaviors that teenagers are trying to keep parents from knowing. When parents suspect what is going on, they need to be tough. But they also should understand that teenagers are at such a vulnerable time in their lives and these young people do not think very well of themselves. They are very compulsive, very driven, and are looking for approval. So parents need to make it very clear that it is the *behavior* they're not happy with, not the teenager. They need to show love and support of the teenager and get beyond the behavior, to demonstrate that they are not rejecting the child, but they are rejecting the behavior."

Parents often ask themselves, "What do I say? How should I tell her?" To ease the anxiety, parents can plan ahead just how they will express their concern in the most beneficial way. It is important to be direct with the child without accusing her or blaming her. Tell her that you are worried about her and that you cannot ignore the symptoms that you have observed. Be direct and honest in describing what you have witnessed. For instance, "I've heard you vomiting after dinner" is more effective than a wishy-washy "You seem to stay in the bathroom for quite a long time each night." Tell her how you feel, what changes you have seen in her attitudes or behaviors, and what worries you. If you phrase your statements from your own viewpoint ("I'm concerned about . . ." or "I have noticed . . ."), you diminish the chances of making indictments (such as *"You're* hurting yourself and all of us" or "What's wrong with *you,* anyway?").

It is important not to judge her feelings for her (as in "You must be terribly unhappy to be doing this to yourself"). If parents label the child's feelings for her or accuse and blame her for the eating disorder and all the havoc it has brought into the family, she will only turn away.

When the parents propose that she get professional help, they may meet strong resistance, particularly if the help is labeled "psychiatric." You may want to phrase the initial suggestion in terms of "seeing the doctor for a medical checkup" because you are concerned about her overall health; you need not harp on her eating behaviors or weight. But however you phrase it, you need to be firm and clear that your daughter has no choice in this matter: an appointment has been made, and she will see the doctor. Because you are concerned about her, you insist that she go.

ANTICIPATING HER RESPONSE

Depending on the type of eating disorder and the individual child's emotions, parents can expect anything from outright denial and rebuke to a sigh of relief that the problem has been recognized.

Anorectics, for the most part, will forcefully deny that they have a medical or psychological problem. They truly believe they are too fat, and they are determined to continue "dieting" even if their weight has dropped to eighty-five pounds or less. When an anorectic is in a starving state, her neurological, metabolic, and hormonal changes interfere with her normal thinking and emotions. She cannot be expected to acknowledge the immediate need for help when she has reached such a state of starvation.

But other anorectics, whose weight has not yet slipped dangerously low, may go along with the notion of seeing a doctor because they do not want to upset their parents. If hospitalization is proposed, a young anorectic may surprisingly comply. "I don't want to hurt my parents anymore, so I'll gain and get out of here" is commonly heard among young hospitalized anorectics. But this initial compliance may not represent a strong, serious commitment to regain weight or to deal with underlying psychological issues.

The anorectic's greatest fear is forced weight gain. "They're afraid of getting fat, and they're afraid that the doctor is going to put them on an uphill track without any ceiling on the weight gain," explains Dr. Slap. "So I try very hard to define and help them accept an appropriate weight goal. I identify for the patient and the family the ideal body weight, and I tell them that I expect this teenager ultimately to reach this weight. I also assure them that I do not want the teenager to exceed that ideal body weight.

"But I make it very clear that as long as she is below 85 percent of ideal body weight, she has active anorexia nervosa and the immediate goal is weight gain. These patients need constant reassurance because they are afraid we're going to make them fat. They are afraid of going to the hospital, of being made to eat, of losing control, of being given calories either through feeding tubes or an IV line. I make it clear that there is some lower limit weight that I just won't accept and that at that weight, we hospitalize them.

"I also make it clear that we are not talking about medical hospitalization alone. We are talking about both medical and psychiatric care, delivered simultaneously via a coordinated eating-disorders program."

Bulimics and compulsive overeaters are often less denying of their problems than anorectics. Though they still maintain outward secrecy about their eating behaviors, many send signals for help, as Jackie did with the toilet bowl brush. The suggestion of going for a medical and psychological evaluation may come as a relief for some bulimics and compulsive overeaters. But they may well be conflicted—while they want help, they also fear and resist giving up their binge-purge cycle. For bulimics who have been secretly bingeing and purging for several years, their eating behavior has become so chronic and self-reinforcing that they can be expected to cling to it like a drowning person to a life raft.

Dr. Bernice L. Rosman, who has researched and written about eating disorders for many years at the Philadelphia Child Guidance Clinic, explains that in the beginning and early stages of these disorders, parents may well focus on the child's emotions that trigger the disorder. But, she cautions, if the eating disorder progresses over time to the chronic stage, the focus needs to shift away from feelings and toward behavior "because the disorder's 'solution' becomes the problem, a rigid habit and, even in the case of bulimic vomiting a kind of addiction which is self-reinforcing. And the struggles around the symptoms [that is, control issues] may then supply new reinforcers to the behavior."

LOCATING A THERAPIST

Unless your pediatrician or family physician has substantial experience in treating eating disorders—and few do at this time—you will need a professional with expertise in the mental health field, specifically with eating disorders. If your doctor cannot recommend one, you could call a nearby hospital, ask for its psychiatry department, and request names of therapists who treat eating disorders.

Or you could call your state or local psychiatric society and request recommendations for eating-disorders specialists. Your phone book may list a local chapter of the American Anorexia/Bulimia Association, which could suggest a list of professionals; if there is no chapter in your area, you can contact the association's national office in New York City at (212) 734-1114 and ask for a list of health-care professionals in your area who are experienced in the treatment of eating disorders. The "Resources" section at the end of this book gives information about other organizations, as well as listing books and videotapes.

A FAMILY APPROACH TO THERAPY

Finding a therapist often confuses parents because there are so many varying approaches to psychotherapy within the profession: psychoanalysis, family therapy, individual therapy, behavior modification, psychopharmacology, support groups, outpatient therapy, and hospital programs.

At the Philadelphia Child Guidance Clinic, which is affiliated with The Children's Hospital of Philadelphia, family therapy is the prevailing approach. This is not to say that other methods are excluded, but treating a young person within the context of his or her family environment has been found to be the most effective there. Because the young person is struggling to grow up and sort out relationships with members of her family, it is vital that family members be involved in and committed to therapy. Equally important is the family's *active* participation in choosing a therapist and *active* involvement in the therapeutic process itself. If a family goes to therapy sessions with the passive expectation that they can sit back, listen, and get the problem solved by a therapist, they will be disappointed in the ineffective results.

Who Is Involved in Family Therapy?

A family approach to therapy does not mean that the entire family goes to every session. But initially, Dr. John Sargent suggests, everyone who lives in the same home with the young person—even the youngest siblings—should meet with the therapist. Although most of his patients are adolescents and young adults, Dr. Sargent's office at the Philadelphia Child Guidance Clinic is stocked with children's blocks, crayons, and toys for the little brothers and sisters.

"Even if they're two years old, the sibling needs to be there for the evaluation in the beginning. The two-year-old knows that things aren't right. So do the five-year-old and the nine-year-old. They know that nobody has been fixing things in the family. All the siblings come to therapy so that they can see the therapist and the parents working together to fix things, so that they get a sense that their own sense of tension, concern, and worry about their sister is ratified.

"Until they come to therapy, their mother has usually been saying, 'Don't worry about it,' but how do they *not* worry if Sister is becoming a skeleton, or she's yelling and screaming or throwing food. That's why siblings need to come—so that their sense that things aren't the way they should be in the family gets supported. They also need to come to therapy so they can stop trying to fix everything themselves. At the dinner table, they'll tell the anorectic to eat, or they'll catch the bulimic bingeing at one A.M. and try to stop her. They need to come to therapy so that they can have a better relationship with their anorectic or bulimic sibling," Dr. Sargent says.

Siblings of children with eating disorders are often called *woodwork children.* They live in the family "woodwork," go about quietly, almost invisibly, and do well socially and academically until they become stressed. When they do get stressed, they do not know what to do because nobody is there to help them. And no one is available to help them because the rest of the family is almost totally focused on their sister's eating disorder.

Professionals in college health services often see these siblings for psychotherapy. "They complain bitterly about all the attention their sister got, about how ineffective their parents were, and they don't feel justified in asking for things for themselves," Dr. Sargent says. "As the anorectic or bulimic becomes increasingly 'special' because of her weird behaviors, the siblings are further distanced from her and from their parents."

The goal for siblings in family therapy is to see that the whole family is working together. "I want them to be here, and I want them to be happy that they're here, that they're part of a family that is trying to fix itself and that is a wonderful, important enterprise. I want them to know that I respect their parents for bringing them and that I respect them for coming," Dr. Sargent says. "I also say that it's not the sibling's job to get Mary to eat or to stop bingeing. I tell the parents to tell the siblings not to tell Mary how to eat. I'll say to the parents, 'Look, you really ought to get Joey to stop telling Mary to eat because he's getting in your way and making things worse for himself and for Mary.'"

Dr. Sargent does the same thing with others who live in the home. "If Grandmom lives with the family, I want her to come in, too, as part of the evaluation. Now, Grandmom may be old, and she is always telling Mary to eat a little more spaghetti; and when Mary doesn't eat, Grandmom is hurt and upset. I tell Mom and Dad to tell Grandmom that 'Mary's eating is *our* business,' that they've got to tell Grandmom that she does not speak about food to the children again. Parents will often say, 'We can't do that. It'll hurt her feelings.' And I'll say, 'Sorry, then I can't help you.'

"When I make a statement like that, I'm not wasting my breath. I'm not making suggestions. This is the treatment. If your child had bacterial meningitis and your pediatrician prescribed antibiotics, you wouldn't disregard it and give her a glass of water instead, would you? No one expects a child to like the taste of medicine, either. I wish the child weren't in this, but she is, and this is the treatment," Dr. Sargent says.

Stepparents and anyone else closely connected to the young person are often part of the evaluation at the beginning of the therapy process. This is important not only to give the therapist as complete a picture as possible of the young person's situation, but also so that everyone understands the mutual goals and learns ways of supporting the young person who has the eating disorder. "It doesn't matter whether the young person with the eating disorder wants the whole family evaluated. It doesn't matter—it is necessary for a complete, coherent evaluation that everyone be present," says Dr. Sargent.

A Team Approach

Wherever you live, whatever services are available to you, and whatever their expense (more on cost at the end of this chapter), you will undoubtedly find that your child's therapy becomes a team effort. The physician who initially examines your child may manage only the medical matters and assign the psychotherapy to a psychiatrist or psychologist. Some eating-disorder programs, particularly those that are hospital-based, involve a physician, a nutritionist or dietitian, and a therapist. As a supplement to individual and family therapy, support groups of young people who are recovering from eating disorders, and their families, can also be of great help.

Regardless of who and how many people are on your therapeutic team, it is vital that everyone involved coordinate their roles and agree on clear delineations of responsibility. As a parent and a consumer of these services, you will need to be an informed, integral member of this team.

The key person on your team will be the therapist because she or he will work most closely with your child. In selecting a therapist, you will want to keep several considerations in mind. You are not shopping for a mechanic to repair your carburetor or a tutor to teach algebra. Skill, experience, and competence are certainly required in any therapist, but your family also must feel comfortable with your therapist. Because treatment will involve not only your child but other members of the family as well, the therapist who will be most effective is one who can establish a relationship of warmth and caring with each individual in the family, who will get to know each one, understand and respect them, and feel connected to each.

If you are troubled at any time by the chemistry between the therapist and your family, you should not hesitate to discuss it with the therapist. Dr. Michael A. Silver of the Philadelphia Child Guidance Clinic says, "Effective therapy for eating disorders is not like surgery or treating pneumonia. It has so much to do with the match between the therapist and the family. In doing family therapy, the therapist should not, for example, blame the parents for the eating problem. But sometimes inadvertently, an impression is created that the parents are at fault, and even before they come in, parents are wondering, 'What have we done wrong?' There is a fine line between recognizing that the parents need to change the way they're handling something—because that way has not been working—and blaming them for the problem. If parents feel that the therapist is blaming them, they should be explicit and say, 'Listen, I feel like you're saying this is my fault,' and discuss it with the therapist. If the parents don't get a sense of satisfaction, they need to find another therapist.

"The flip side," Dr. Silver continues, "is that parents may inadvertently be doing things that aren't helping and that are making the problem worse, though that is not their intention. They may get the sense that the therapist is pussyfooting around, not calling them on something. If the parents feel the therapist is not willing to challenge them, that is disrespectful as well. If you are going to trust the therapist, the therapist needs to be able to respectfully challenge you about things that are going on without either blaming or overlooking."

Making It Work

From the outset of therapy, certain ingredients must be in place for the therapeutic team to succeed most effectively:

- The family senses that the therapist is not only knowledgeable about eating disorders in general but understands this family's own unique situation.
- The therapist conveys that understanding in such a way that points to a direction, a plan, and a goal.
- Family and therapist alike recognize that nobody is being blamed for the eating disorder. Blame is not the issue.
- The therapist promotes and supports everyone's involvement in therapy, while also making it clear that they will be asked at different times in the course of therapy to do different things.
- The therapist is not a judge, jury, minister, priest, or rabbi. A therapist is someone who helps people change, a catalyst.

"Family therapy really means that the family trusts the therapist, supports the girl's going to therapy, supports her working with the therapist, and goes themselves if they have questions about what the girl is doing," urges Dr. Sargent. "It's the family's responsibility—particularly because they're paying for it—to make certain that the individual session works to their advantage. And that advantage is that their daughter grows up as independently and successfully as she can. Parents want to make sure that the therapist has the same goal as they have, which is to help their daughter grow up. And they want to make sure that the therapy is not supporting her being immature, indecisive, or whatever is hindering her maturing."

Setting Goals

Each therapist and family will set individual goals, of course, but everyone involved needs to understand them clearly and agree upon strategies to reach them. In Sheila's case, one of the family's initial goals was to remove their emphasis on Sheila's food.

Before they began therapy, Sheila's family had been so intent on making her eat that every mealtime became an exercise in tension. Her parents and older sister carped at her about each morsel.

"You're eating just the white of the egg! Why can't you eat the yolk, too?"

"How many calories can possibly be in that salad, twenty?"

"Just eat one more bite, dear, just a little more, please. How can that possibly make you fat?"

Sheila ignored these proddings, excused herself from the table, or argued with them until everyone had knots in their stomachs and no one wanted to finish the meal.

But as one of their first goals in therapy, Sheila's family agreed not to discuss Sheila's weight or what or how little she ate, and they were not to hover over her, watching each forkful that went into her mouth.

After months of doing just that every day, this was quite a difficult pattern to break, and they had to remind themselves repeatedly not to butt in. At the same time, they recognized that Sheila, the doctor monitoring her physical health, and their psychotherapist had agreed that she was to stop losing weight and begin gaining gradually toward a minimally acceptable weight.

If Sheila appeared not to be eating at home, the family tried not to jump on her during mealtimes. Instead, her mother or father reminded her of her commitment during calm nonmealtimes. If she still seemed to restrict her food intake, they would bring up the matter at the next therapy session. While that was the agreed-upon strategy, there were many times when one parent or her sister fell back into the old routine: "Eat this, Sheila, it's delicious! Why don't you try just a little?" But over time and with conscious effort, these regressions diminished in frequency and intensity.

New Ways to Solve Old Problems

The goal of therapy is not simply to help the young person abandon her eating disorder but to help her find new solutions to the underlying emotional problems that have led to the starving, bingeing-purging, or compulsive overeating. An effective therapist will guide the young person and her family toward new ways of making relationships—with themselves, with each other, and with friends and peers.

"What I try to do," explains Dr. Sargent, "is help them find a way of living without the eating-disordered behavior, and that generally requires that they solve relationship problems, problems about achievement, and problems about friendships and sexuality—and that they solve these problems in a different way and more overtly. Treatment is all about finding whichever of these relationship issues resonates with people and, at the same time, paying attention to the physical needs of the young person.

"We're treating the person, not the disorder, and the person is ultimately more important than the symptoms," Dr. Sargent continues. "Her symptoms are a sign of discomfort, and the reasons for that discomfort are inherent in her situation: her family, school, and community. We are not asking, 'Why is she eating so much (or so little)?' but rather, 'Why isn't she doing something else?' If she's so uncomfortable that she's got to numb herself with food, let's find out why she's so uncomfortable."

If therapy is to be effective, everyone's cooperation and collaboration are needed. At the outset of treatment, each participant is involved with the therapist in setting goals, and throughout the course of treatment, each is responsible for following through. It is essential for the young person, the therapist, and every family member to work together toward accomplishing the same thing. But what is that "same thing"? Is it that she put on weight or stop bingeing? No, it goes beyond the outward symptom of the eating disorder. It goes to the heart of the matter, which is something of a balancing act. On one end of this balance beam, the family is being maintained; the family unit is held together in a commitment to therapy, to helping the affected young person. On the other end, each individual member of the family is beginning to change, to become more individually differentiated and less self-critical.

As therapy proceeds and various family issues are addressed, each family member's statements are taken seriously because, in order for therapy to work, the relationships built in the process must be based on honesty, straightforwardness, and accountability. In other words, when someone says he will do something, he is expected to do it.

"That becomes extraordinarily difficult when one has a thirteen-year-old, five-foot-three, seventy-five-pound young woman who is saying that she doesn't have any problems and that she just needs to lose a few more pounds," says Dr. Sargent. "Then the question becomes, How do you involve her in the treatment process and in the treatment contract? My sense is that you involve her by allowing her to save face, by allowing her to believe what she believes, while at the same time helping her parents to help her stay safe. That safety is based upon the achievement of slow-to-modest gradual weight gain.

"And that safety is also based on an appreciation of her feelings and her discomfort. It's fine for her not to *want* to gain weight, but it's just not fine for her *not* to gain weight. The expectation is that she follow through, but she is allowed to maintain disagreement."

The family is asked to make a clear separation between how they respond to her feelings and to her behavior. They respond to her feelings with support ("I understand," "I hear you"), but they respond to her behavior with sanctions or direction. "This is often precisely what hasn't been happening in her past," Dr. Sargent says. "The family has been previously responding to her feelings with sanctions and to her behavior with no guidance."

To reverse the old pattern can be threatening and upsetting for some families because they have long been trying to *make* her happy and satisfied. But it is not the family's job to make her happy. The family's job is to help her find ways of making herself happy.

The Treatment Symphony

Dr. Sargent compares treatment to a symphony. "If you listen," he says, "a symphony has an opening exploration of various themes, a middle section where the themes are worked out, and a final section where the themes are summarized, clarified, and stated once more. Perhaps at the end, the themes are made clear and in such a way that is different and demonstrates growth.

"If you think about treatment, the initial phase is one in which the family as a whole meets with the therapist and decides about goals. In the process, the therapist identifies and forms a relationship with each individual at the same time he's meeting with the family. Then the middle phase of treatment is an opportunity for each family member, through identifying their own goals, to resolve conflicts with other family members so that family life is more satisfying, so that individuals are more differentiated and more successful, and so that people are appreciated for what they feel and who they are, as well as for what they do."

In Dr. Sargent's experience, as well as that of many others who treat eating disorders, the therapist works in different ways with the father-daughter relationship and the mother-daughter relationship. In the father-daughter relationship, the therapist "allows for both feelings and actions, allows for choices, and for sharing control," Dr. Sargent explains. "The therapist recognizes the tremendous importance of this girl to this father and this father to this girl. Meanwhile, the therapist helps the father to develop his own sense of self-esteem. And that is the key because every parent I've met whose child has an eating disorder doubts themselves, wonders why this has happened to them, and feels like a failure. Every one of us has had circumstances in which we've failed to meet our aspirations. It seems to me that the goal of the therapist is to help people recognize that just because they have a problem now doesn't mean that they're bad people, that criticism can be constructive rather than personally damaging, and that ultimately people can decide what they want to do with their relationships.

"With the mother-daughter relationship," Dr. Sargent continues, "the important thing is the process of rapprochement, which means that each of them recognizes her importance to the other. One of the most important things a mother can do, in the course of treatment, is to come to believe in and respect her own life, because if she doesn't believe in and respect her own life, she will not be able to pass that kind of feeling along to her daughter."

In the family therapy that Dr. Sargent and others practice, the family is seen as a cohesive unit, but one composed of very different individuals—in other words, family members are both connected and separate. Sheila, for example, came to recognize in the course of her family therapy that she could both love and hate her parents at the same time. She could remain loyal to her family, but she also could hate her father for moving them around and for denying her unhappiness about it. She could love her mother and, at the same time, distance herself from her mother's own unhappiness about the family's nomadlike existence.

Connection and Separation

As the young person and her family proceed through therapy, each comes to realize that connection to and separation from one another are equally important. While the young woman grows more independent and mature, her parents grow more respectful of her choices. They begin to offer support and caring without control. As she strives to become more self-reliant, she may also seek her parents' and the therapist's help. This calls for mutual support. "True mutual support," Dr. Sargent says, "means we will work together, we'll collaborate. I will respect you, and you can tell me what is not right, and I will tell you what I think isn't right. People need to be able to ask for help, and that help should be provided in a way that helps rather than controls."

To illustrate that point, Dr. Sargent draws upon his own childhood: "I loved to work with my dad, and one of the things he'd let me do was help him paint. When I was about eight years old, I was painting a door. If you've ever painted a door, you know it's difficult to do it without the brushstrokes showing. One brushstroke creates other brushstrokes, and so forth. I was having trouble and couldn't get it to look smooth, so I said to my dad, 'I'm having trouble here.' My dad took the brush away from me and fixed it in about five minutes.

"I felt little, criticized, and insignificant because I had not been helped. The thing had been taken away from me. The help had controlled rather than helped. And I think that's the key in therapy: we need to find a way to help people that feels like help and support, not control."

Different Approaches for Anorexia and Bulimia

Although addressing and altering relationships lies at the heart of treatment for both anorexia and bulimia, therapy approaches differ for each of these eating disorders, depending on the young person's age, the length of time she has been engaged in the eating disorder, and the nature of the disorder itself.

THERAPY FOR THE ANORECTIC. For the anorectic, treatment "will often involve her gaining weight and then owning her own body as an adolescent in a way that she hasn't done before," Dr. Sargent explains. "It will involve her owning peer relationships, activities, heterosexual relationships, her school and social performance, as well as her food. It may take six to twelve months or longer."

If she has lost a significant amount of weight, the anorectic's treatment may require hospitalization to regain the necessary weight and to enable her to begin dealing with the psychological aspects of her disorder. Gaining enough weight to begin menstruating "becomes a real flag of progress," Dr. Gail B. Slap says. "That is the minimal acceptable weight, and this often becomes a point of discussion and conflict." It is difficult to give a young woman a precise weight at which she will resume menstruation. "It's easier to give her a certain percentage of body fat, but she does not measure her percent of body fat every day—she stands on a scale," Dr. Slap explains. "So I try to provide some assessment of body fat and to explain its correlation to weight and menstruation."

Whether she is hospitalized or not, Dr. Sargent stresses, "there is a tremendous need for intense involvement of the family in adolescent anorexia. With early-onset anorectics [those whose anorexia first appears in preadolescence or the early teens], I am interested in obliterating the symptom as a choice. Teaching the young teenager this is vital: We're going to help you get over this symptom, and we're going to do it quickly and straightforwardly. We're going to remind you that this restrictive eating behavior is not an option. And the whole family's involvement here is essential."

In the case of older anorectics whose weight has fluctuated up and down for years, though always remaining lower than ideal, Dr. Sargent explains that such "chronic anorexia is probably best treated through individual therapy with family support. It may continue through adulthood without necessarily recovery from being thin. It may be that chronic anorexia is a life-style. For example, a woman's minimal normal weight might be 125, but she usually weighs about 112. Maybe she feels more comfortable when she gets down around 102, and maybe when she's very stressed she drops to 95, and later her weight will rise again. With these older anorectics, we do a different approach—we're not interested that they eat ice cream to put on weight, but more interested in helping them get into graduate school, solve a job or relationship problem, or whatever is going on in their adult lives." But if the anorectic is younger and living at home, parental involvement in therapy is essential.

THERAPY FOR THE BULIMIC OR COMPULSIVE OVEREATER. For the bulimic or compulsive overeater, therapy may differ somewhat, depending on age, duration of the disorder, and whether the young person lives with her family. Bulimics like Jackie, for instance, may binge and purge occasionally in high school, but once they leave home and enter college or get a job, the frequency of their bulimia intensifies. Often these young women receive therapy on an individual basis, through a college or community health service, and their families are not directly involved.

"The key to treating bulimia is not to get rid of bulimia, but for the bulimic to *own* her own symptoms," Dr. Sargent believes. "Because as soon as she says, 'Yes, I really want to overeat, and I love to throw up,' then she wonders about it. Then she can choose something else. In a sense, it's very similar to the beginning process for treatment of alcoholism, which is the recognition that, 'Yes, I am someone who has this capacity, who digs this; this is something that's part of me; it has consequences, and I take responsibility for that. Then I can choose whether I do it or not.'

"But bulimia can be difficult to treat," he continues, "because people are highly ambivalent about the symptom. They like it. The symptom does something for them. It's different for each individual. Some say, 'It's mine—I have something that's mine.' Some like the feeling of doing something unusual. Some like the fact that they're living on the edge. It can be a catch-22—the young person comes in and says 'Here are the symptoms; take them away, Doctor. But if you touch them, I'm outta here.' If the doctor doesn't take them away, he's seen as incompetent and ineffective. But if he touches them, he's told, 'Back off. You're abusing me.'

"That is the inherent paradox: 'If you care about me, you'd recognize that I'm out of control and that I need you to control me; but if you really cared about me, you would recognize that I'm an independent person with my own autonomy, and under no circumstances will someone who respects me try to control me.' It's a can't-win situation.

"What the doctor then does, since he or she can't win, is to affiliate with the person and say, 'It's yours. Tell me how to help. Tell me what you want from me.'" The therapist also has to be careful to open the door without dragging the young person through it because, as Dr. Sargent explains, "Many of the people we see for eating disorders, particularly bulimics, have a lot of trouble with boundaries. If they let you know too much about themselves, they then get scared and retreat too far."

When Jackie first met with her therapist, she offered a few sketchy details about her bingeing and purging. The following portion of their dialogue shows how an effective therapist can establish a helpful relationship from the outset:

Therapist: How can I help you, Jackie?

Jackie: I don't know if you can. I don't know if I want you to, really.

Therapist: I don't know if I can help you, but I know a lot about the problem. You're going to have to teach me about you. I need you to be seeing a doctor so that I know that you're physically safe while you're here at college. And if you're not safe, then you're going to have to go

> home, and we're not going to be able to
> work together. But if you can keep
> yourself physically safe, we'll work
> together.

The therapist's straightforward opening allowed Jackie to sense that she could trust him. Over time, she did teach him about herself, and he guided her toward the self-discovery that she indeed "owned" her bulimia, that she was responsible for it, and that once she acknowledged that, she could make other choices about her life.

CONSUMER ISSUES

Three final points must be made before moving on to the next chapter about the recovery process. All three points are part of the "be a smart consumer" issue.

Therapy can be very costly and lengthy. If your child requires hospitalization, you can anticipate considerable expense and hope that your medical insurance covers it. If your medical plan does not cover psychotherapy, you could talk to a hospital social worker to explore other possible ways of financing therapy. Aside from hospital costs, outpatient psychotherapy is expensive. The cost of a session with a therapist may range from $50 to $100 an hour in various locations. Some therapists offer a sliding scale based on your ability to pay. Families need to be prepared for this expense and for the eventuality that there may be many, many sessions.

At the beginning of therapy, parents often ask how long the therapeutic process will take. The duration obviously depends on each individual's needs, but it is safe to generalize that therapy is no quick magic bullet. "Oftentimes the process of helping the adolescent take responsibility for her own appetites, behaviors, need for involvement with others, and her need for autonomy, takes a long time," Dr. Sargent notes.

At the outset, it is helpful to discuss both the estimated cost and the anticipated length of treatment with the therapist and to understand his or her policies on scheduling and canceling appointments. Some therapists, for example, expect payment for a missed session if it is not canceled within a specified time period.

The second point: You may have read or heard from other parents that antidepressant drugs are sometimes administered for eating disorders. Only physicians and psychiatrists can prescribe these, of course, not psychologists or other non-medically trained counselors. The use of antidepressants is not universal. They tend to be prescribed more often for bulimics than for anorectics, but in either situation parents will want to discuss thoroughly their possible use with the physician. You will want to understand fully the doctor's reasons for prescribing the medication, what the anticipated result may be, what the dosage is, what possible side effects may appear, and the likely duration of the medication's course.

The third point is the blunt and disturbing fact that a few young women have been victimized by their therapists. Certainly the vast majority of therapists are highly ethical, but a small number have taken advantage of vulnerable, lonely young women who want to feel love. In their relationships with other people, many of these patients have come to believe that they must trade their looks, achievements, or sexuality for love. In their experience, Dr. Sargent explains, "they have learned that it's only as long as they have something to trade that they get back what they want." In striving to receive warmth and acceptance, some of these young women have become involved in inappropriate relationships with their therapists.

Parents need to be aware of this, but they should not use it as an excuse to resist treatment. Our intent here is certainly not to promote distrust of therapists. Trust is an essential ingredient in a therapeutic relationship, but that trust should not be blind. Nor are we suggesting therapist-shopping. Changing therapists blithely is not wise. In fact, it can be detrimental and disruptive to a child because each time, she must begin all over again to establish another relationship with a new therapist. But if parents are disturbed by their daughter's involvement with a therapist, they should discuss their concerns openly with the therapist and consider the therapist's responses. If they are not satisfied, they need to find another therapist.

CHAPTER 9

Toward Recovery

Once a young person begins treatment for an eating disorder, her parents are often relieved because the problem has been recognized and professional help has begun. Their hopes are high. A speedy, total recovery is just around the corner, parents want to believe.

Parents deserve a sigh of relief—they have taken a courageous step in enlisting help for their child and for themselves. They should congratulate themselves for engaging in therapy. But this initial euphoria should be tempered by the long view. The road to recovery requires hard work of everyone involved, and there will likely be pitfalls, places where you will feel "stuck" without signs of progress, and perhaps a few relapses. High hopes will gradually evolve into realistic expectations: your child can get better, but recovery takes a long time and much effort. Finally, when therapy nears conclusion, there will be fear: "She has come such a long way, but how will she do on her own, without the safety net of therapy?" one mother worried.

If there is a key phrase to guide parents along the road toward recovery, it may be *flexibility with firmness.* Over the course of effective therapy, not only will the young person change, but each member of the family will change in relationship to her. Flexibility is essential for everyone to grow and change, while firmness—not rigidity—is equally necessary to support her recovery.

LEARNING ANOTHER LANGUAGE

Throughout the course of therapy, it is helpful for families to remind themselves of a basic understanding about eating disorders: The symptoms of the disorder (whether they are restrictive eating, fanatical exercising, or bingeing and purging) have become a *language,* a way of communicating, within the family. The symptoms may be saying, "I'm hurting," "I want to be in control of my life, but I don't know how," "I love you, Mom and Dad, but I want to be separate from you, too," or "I'm afraid." In turn, parents may answer the symptoms with bewilderment, attempts to control, sanctions, or anger.

To change that language, individuals within the family are encouraged through therapy to communicate more directly through words. That means that the young person will learn to communicate her feelings verbally, while her family will learn to drop the old predictable responses to her symptoms and to communicate their feelings verbally as well. For instance, instead of responding to a bulimic with a barrage of orders to stop bingeing, a parent might substitute statements such as, "I'm really upset by all the food missing from the kitchen. I don't enjoy being so mad at you, and I want to help. If you'd like to talk about it, I'm ready to listen whenever you like."

Statements like these, which honestly express your feelings

but do not criticize, blame, accuse, or indict, can encourage her to open up and communicate more directly with you. And even if her verbal communication is surprisingly hostile, it is a step toward recovery. She is moving away from using her disorder's symptoms as her "language" and toward a more open, honest communication by expressing her feelings through words.

BRIDGING YOUR EXPERIENCES

Parents who have been through the treatment and recovery process look back and often advise other families to keep another thought in mind: When you are living through this, it is helpful to reassure yourself that your child is not bizarre or crazy—though her behaviors may be. She is a human being with whom you have many things in common, things you may have forgotten or overlooked. If you can bridge your experiences with hers to form a common ground of shared experiences, you can help form a sound basis for new, healthier relationships. Jackie's mother was able to do this by recalling some of her own teenage fears and anxieties and talking about them with Jackie. When you are able to do this, your responses to your child can become more empathic and will less likely be rejected by her.

But there is a fine line here. While you are sharing your similar experiences, you also learn to recognize her uniqueness and your own, her individuality and your own, her autonomy and your own. As parent and child get to know each other in new ways through family therapy, there will be both connection and separation of the individuals. Just as the parent cannot live vicariously through the child, the child needs to see the parent as a unique, separate person. This is essential if she is to have a good role model for growing up.

"Just Tell Us What to Do"

When families set out on the road to recovery, they often hope that the therapist will give them a neat handbook, something like the Automobile Association of America might give a traveler, with routes highlighted on the roadmaps and recommended stopovers for each destination. While it is true that the therapist, young person, and family members need to establish clear goals at the beginning of treatment, parents cannot expect a concise set of techniques or rules to direct them toward those goals or to guarantee that they will reach them. This is not a board game with a rule book tucked inside the box. The discovery that change and recovery will not be attained through precise guidelines is frustrating and discomfiting for many families.

One father explained that he wanted to tell the therapist, "Look, Doc, we brought her in here to see you. We're paying your fee. Now just tell us what to do. Give us the recipe for making her get well." When he realized that therapy would not provide exact ABC techniques to follow, he felt anxious and annoyed. But by the end of his daughter's treatment, he looked back and realized that such a muddy start was actually the only possible way he and his family could have begun to change their relationships. They needed to explore, like a backpacking family lost in a forest without a clearly marked trail. They needed to bump into the trees and into each other. They needed to hit some dead ends and retrace their steps in circles a few times in order to find their way out of the woods. If every third tree bore a trail marking, their path would have been too simple: they would have followed it almost blindly, and they would have discovered nothing about themselves.

Some Points to Keep in Mind

There is always a caveat, of course! While each family needs to be flexible because there are no lockstep techniques for everyone, parents can bear in mind some general perspectives throughout therapy and recovery.

Your Child's Fears

Your child will likely feel frightened because therapy requires her to change. Until now, her eating disorder has helped her cope with or survive her emotional discomfort. It has been her way of controlling the demons in her life—and perhaps her way of manipulating other people. Now therapy is challenging her to surrender those coping methods and to find healthier substitutes. She is being asked to give up symptoms that have been working for her, that have given her a measure of security, as strange as they appear to the rest of the world. She is being asked to try something very new and risky, something unknown that frightens her. Like you, she may wish that there were a clear set of techniques for recovery, but she too will have to be flexible, to test the untested path, and to yield some security and control for an unpredictable journey toward an end she cannot envision. She will feel helpless and lost much of the time, just as you will.

The Paradox of Disengagement

As much as you want to comfort her in her struggle, you may be simultaneously agonized. You want to jump in and rescue her, but you feel helpless. Simply being aware that this is a normal part of the therapeutic process can be of some help, but it is equally important to recognize a paradox: Though you are riveted on her struggle to overcome her disorder, you need to focus *less* on it. You are not her therapist. You can only recognize that she is going through the most trying challenge of her young life. You can be there for her, you can make yourself available to her, but you cannot force her to change or make her even wish to change. You cannot "cure" her or take her symptoms away for her. She must work through this herself with the help of a therapist and with your emotional support—but not with your dominance or overinvolvement in her disorder.

"Isn't that contradictory?" you might ask. "How can I show support and be uninvolved at the same time?" It *is* a difficult balancing act, but therapists caution that it is crucial to recovery that parents and other loved ones separate from the young person, that they demonstrate their support and commitment to her recovery, but that they also disengage from her so that she can move toward her own autonomy. Parents can help her do that in two ways.

MAINTAINING SELF-AWARENESS. Think about her struggle and ask yourself, "How do I feel about her eating disorder? How does it affect me?" "What does her eating disorder say about our family relationships?" "Are her outward behaviors, which so anger and frustrate us, a manipulation to make us feel guilty? Are they a search for love and approval? A way of carving herself an identity?" Based on the answers you find to these questions, ask yourself two more: "What does this reveal about the way we communicate in our family?" "Where do we share common issues and concerns?" These introspective questions will come up during therapy, but they need not be held until the next week's session before you reflect on them. They may come to you at any time, and there may be an unexpected moment when you can discuss them with your spouse.

TAKING TIME OUT. A second way to help your child move toward autonomy is to take time for yourself. Plan your day and your week around your own needs, not your child's. Your emotional and physical needs should not take a back seat to hers, even though her disorder has forced itself to the front and center of the family stage. If daily family routines are set by her binge-purge cycles or by her rigid mealtime routines, it is important to reschedule family life more normally, as Sheila's family has begun to do since beginning therapy. When her family is planning to go to a seven-thirty movie, they will now eat dinner at six, whether Sheila joins them or not. If she wants to make them an elaborate meal that will take two hours to prepare (though she will eat little of it), her family no longer caves in to her demand. They simply tell her that they will fix a quicker meal and will eat it at a designated time. If she joins them, that is fine. If she does not, they go ahead and eat it anyway.

Sheila fought their attempts to return to normalcy from time to time, but she needed to learn that a sense of balance had to return to her family's life, that clear-cut boundaries were necessary to give each family member an identity and a role, and that her eating disorder would no longer dominate family life. As their therapist suggested, it was important for Sheila to see steadiness in those around her in order for her to learn that her family was strong enough to withstand the turmoil that she had been acting out through her eating disorder.

Parents who have been through this, as well as professionals, urge parents to take time for themselves, to have fun just for the sake of enriching their own lives. That advice may seem flip when your child is starving or bingeing and vomiting, but it is meant seriously. An eating disorder can pull every member of the family into quicksand. The child's condition can be so all-consuming that parents never allow themselves to take an evening off for dinner with friends, to see a movie, or even to take a relaxed stroll through the park. Those small events are vital to maintaining their own well-being. If parents deny themselves fun or a break, they are not only hurting themselves, but they are also feeding into the child's condition. She needs to see the members of her family getting on with their lives, coping, and hopefully even having a few laughs from time to time. And when she can join a family activity or outing that gives pleasure and enjoyment, all the better for everyone.

WHAT YOU MAY EXPECT

Many families who are beginning therapy wish they had a crystal ball to predict how it will progress, how long it will last, and how it will turn out a year or so from now. There is nothing magical or predictable about therapy, but from others' experiences, a few general observations can be made.

Early Changes in the Symptoms

Near the beginning of therapy, a young person's symptoms may appear to be worse rather than better. A bulimic, for instance, may binge and purge even more frequently in an effort to grasp the symptom tightly before surrendering it. Like the raggedy old teddy bear she has snuggled since infancy, she hugs the familiar, comforting symptom one last time before relinquishing it. This does not always happen, of course, but it should not come as a surprise if it does. An anorectic, too, who had always been a complacent child may become sullen or testy in the early months of therapy. Her parents may question whether therapy is helping her, but they should understand that this again is not unusual. Therapy is new and frightening for her. She fears she will be forced to gain unwanted pounds, and she is discovering feelings previously hidden.

For some bulimics or compulsive overeaters, their bingeing may seem to decrease markedly soon after they enter therapy. Debby's parents, for example, thought they had found the magic cure when she almost abruptly stopped bingeing after her second or third session with a therapist. But this can be a false sign of progress because many people later resume their eating-disordered behaviors when therapy begins to shed light on the sources of their underlying emotional distress. Facing those emotions directly for the first time is frightening, particularly if they have been pent up for a long time. These apparent "relapses" are a signal that she is working hard at therapy; they are not unusual and should not be a cause of major concern as long as she remains committed to continuing therapy.

Relapses

Relapses may occur particularly after therapy has ended when the young person goes through a significant life change: breaking up with a boyfriend, leaving one school and entering another, graduating from high school and facing college or a job, moving away from home. She may need to touch base with her therapist for a while again during these transitional stages of her life. Support and self-help groups can also help her at these times.

Hospitalization

In situations where the young person requires hospitalization, it is important for her family to recognize that hospitalization is not a judgment of their failure or a relinquishing of their responsibility for her. Instead, it is an opportunity for the whole family to learn new methods of responding to her symptoms and supporting her recovery. This is not easy, but the young person and the family have the support of physicians, therapists, nurses, nutritionists, and dietitians who share their goal—that the young person become independent, competent, and self-satisfied. At the same time, the family is acquiring insights and skills through the therapist, who acts as a catalyst, to help each other grow and change.

When hospitalization is required, it is important to recognize the contradictory feelings the young person probably has about it. She may hate being there, or she may feel shame and guilt for being hospitalized. Yet she may also feel safe in that protective environment where, as one young anorectic explained it, "I don't have to worry constantly about what my parents will tell me to eat, or how I'll hurt their feelings if I don't eat it, or how I'll sneak it off my plate and into the garbage."

Feelings of Improvement

As signs of improvement occur (the anorectic gradually regains weight; the bulimic and compulsive overeater's binges diminish in frequency and amount of food consumed), parents may expect their child to feel better. But that does not necessarily follow. The young person may be getting better but not feeling better. She is uncomfortable with new feelings and is learning to explore and tolerate discomforting ones. As the bulimic, for example, learns to ride out or resist an urge to binge, she feels extremely anxious. This is difficult and scary for her because, before therapy, she raced to food as soon as she experienced any emotional upset. Now she is trying to hold off, to keep that urge at arm's length for a while and see if it will pass while she tries to calm herself without bingeing. It is no wonder she does not *feel* instantly better, but she is *getting* better.

Concerns About the Therapist

From time to time throughout therapy, the young person or individual family members may become distressed or impatient with the therapist. As mentioned in Chapter 8, it is important to air these concerns directly with the therapist. But it is also necessary to understand that the therapist's role is that of a catalyst. The therapist is not doing an effective job if he or she does not challenge the family to change, and this can be uncomfortable.

THERAPY IN THREE ACTS

Therapy can be viewed as something of a three-act play. In the first act, problems are identified, goals are set, and initial progress is made with the physical aspects of the eating disorder: the anorectic stops losing and begins slowly to gain some weight, or the bulimic or compulsive overeater binges less frequently.

During the second act, the therapist shifts the focus toward the psychological problems that are inhibiting the young person's development and toward unresolved family conflicts. If the parents are not expecting this shift of focus, they may say, "Whoa—why are we talking about other people in the family? Aren't we here to help solve our daughter's eating problem?" They are, of course, but it is also essential to identify stresses within family life that may have contributed to that problem and to find other ways of coping with stress.

As these psychological conflicts are explored, family members may experience anger, shame, guilt, or hostility toward each other and a host of other agitating emotions. At these moments the therapist helps the young person understand, perhaps for the first time in her life, that disagreements between parent and child, husband and wife, brother and sister, are part of life. Recognizing that each person in the family is a separate and distinct individual can be a painful process, but everyone needs to partake in the process in order for the young person to develop autonomy, to solve her problems independently, and to take responsibility for herself.

A therapist also assists during these upseting times by modeling negotiation and compromise skills for the young person and the rest of the family. He or she encourages the young person to speak up and be assertive and challenges her to find strategies for working out conflicts with her parents, to accept mistakes and disappointments, and to become less rigid in her view of her weight and body shape.

In interacting with parents, a therapist will likely steer them away from overinvolvement and toward disengagement from the child with the eating disorder. Marital therapy may also be suggested as a way for parents to reflect on their own needs and relationship. A supportive therapist will not accuse or blame the parents but will focus on mutual support, compromise, and negotiation within the marriage, and he or she will strongly discourage parents from dragging their children into their own disagreements. In the midst of exploring family conflicts, parents may occasionally consider marital separation, but many therapists discourage it at this time and suggest that the husband and wife delay such a decision until their child's therapy is further along. In the midst of treatment, their primary responsibility is their child's recovery. If they eventually do decide to separate, the therapist can help them do so in ways that will have the least harmful effects on the family. The therapist can also help the children respond to the separation.

TOWARD TERMINATION

Therapy's third and final act leads toward termination of treatment. Individual family members do not all get up from their chairs and walk out the door together, however. Frequently there are follow-up sessions every few months once the young person's eating problems have diminished and the family is functioning more effectively. Even after follow-ups are concluded, telephone contact may continue intermittently.

The end of therapy is rarely clear-cut or final. It never occurs as crisply as tearing a page off the calendar. An anorectic's weight may have risen to an acceptable level, but she may have yet to develop fully other means of solving her problems. She may stay in therapy for months beyond the apparent "cure" of her self-starvation. Her family may have begun to resolve family difficulties and to make productive changes in their own lives. The frequency of their meetings with the therapist may dwindle to one every month or six weeks and eventually cease altogether, though their daughter still sees the therapist individually as needed.

A bulimic or compulsive overeater may not have binged for three months but is still working on ways of relating to others in her life, ways that will help her manage stressful situations without falling back into the binge-purge cycle. For her, too, therapy may continue much longer, as long as she feels the need for support, long after she is functioning at a more independent, steady pace. Her therapy may taper off from weekly sessions with her therapist to occasional follow-ups and monthly support-group meetings with other recovering bulimics.

"Coming out of therapy is scary," Jackie's mother said soon after her daughter, their family, and the therapist all concluded that Jackie had her symptoms under control, had learned new ways of communicating with them, and had found new ways of handling stress in her life.

"I was really anxious when we realized she'd soon stop seeing the therapist. My shoulders are only so wide. I've been carrying a lot, trying to change my own life, too, and therapy has helped lift some of the burden off my shoulders," her mother said. "As long as Jackie has been going to see the therapist, I knew a safety net is there to catch her if anything goes wrong. But remove that safety net, and I admit I'm anxious. On the other hand, we've all learned so much about ourselves and each other that I know we're stronger and more able to cope because of therapy."

Once Jackie's therapy formally ended, she continued to attend a support group of young people who were recovering from eating disorders. At the same time, her mother attended a support group for parents whenever she felt the need for encouragement from others who had traveled the same road.

Just as family members collaborate on setting goals at the beginning of the treatment process, everyone involved needs to make certain that all parts of the therapy fit together like a completed jigsaw puzzle at the conclusion of therapy. While the treatment process may formally end with the young person's abolishing her eating-disordered behaviors, individual family members may benefit by individual therapy in the future, as part of their own personal growth.

Although this book ends here, it may be just the beginning of your child's recovery. You have recognized the problem.

You are facing it directly. You have been through much pain, and you will undoubtedly feel more pain as you work toward healing. But you are not alone. If you have not done so already, you will find a therapist with whom you will collaborate. Together, your family, your child, and your therapist can begin this journey with the knowledge that your love for your child and your courage in facing this challenge will lead you toward a clearer understanding of your child, her problems, and your own. And that understanding will give each of you great strength and comfort.

Notes

1. Yates, Alayne, M.D. "Current Perspectives on the Eating Disorders," *Journal of The American Academy of Child and Adolescent Psychiatry* 28 (1989): 813.

2. Lasegue, E. C., "On Hysterical Anorexia," *Medical Times Gazette* 2 (1873): 265.

3. Rockwell, W. K. Kenneth, M.D., "Evaluation and Treatment of Eating Disorders," *Clinical Advances in the Treatment of Psychiatric Disorders* 2 (Nov./Dec. 1988): 3.

4. Herzog, David B., M.D., and Paul M. Copeland, M.D., "Eating Disorders," *New England Journal of Medicine* 313 (Aug. 1, 1985): 295.

5. Minuchin, Salvador, Bernice L. Rosman, and Lester Baker, *Psychosomatic Families: Anorexia Nervosa in Context* (Cambridge: Harvard University Press, 1978).

6. Boskind-White, Marlene, and William C. White, Jr., *Bulimarexia: The Binge/Purge Cycle* (New York: W.W. Norton, 1983), 137.

7. Roth, Geneen, *Feeding the Hungry Heart: The Experience of Compulsive Overeating* (Indianapolis and New York: Bobbs-Merrill, 1982), 93–94.

Resources

The following lists of books, videotapes, and organizations may be helpful to parents who wish to learn more about eating disorders and obesity. The list is intended not to be comprehensive but to serve as a starting point for finding further information. Your local library can also be helpful in locating material about eating disorders.

BOOKS

Ardell, Maureen, and Corry-Ann Ardell. *Portrait of an Anorexic: A Mother and Daughter's Story.* Vancouver: Flight Press, 1985.

Bruch, Hilde, M.D. *Eating Disorders: Obesity, Anorexia Nervosa, and the Person Within.* New York: Basic Books, 1973.

Bruch, Hilde, M.D. *The Golden Cage: The Enigma of Anorexia Nervosa.* New York: Vintage Books, 1979 (originally published by Harvard University Press, 1978).

Brumberg, Joan Jacobs. *Fasting Girls: The History of Anorexia Nervosa.* New York: New American Library, 1988.

Byrne, Catherine. *A Parent's Guide to Anorexia and Bulimia.* New York: Henry Holt, 1987.

Chernin, Kim. *The Hungry Self: Women, Eating and Identity.* New York: Times Books, 1985.

Chernin, Kim. *The Obsession: Reflections on the Tyranny of Slenderness.* New York: Harper and Row, 1981.

Clark, Kristine, Richard Parr, and William Castelli, eds. *Evaluation and Management of Eating Disorders: Anorexia, Bulimia, and Obesity.* LaCrosse Exercise and Health Series. Champaign, Ill.: Life Enhancement Publications, 1988.

Collipp, Platon J., M.D., ed. *Childhood Obesity.* New York: Warner Books, 1986.

Dowling, Colette. *Perfect Women.* New York: Summit Books, 1988.

Epstein, Leonard H., and Sally Squires. *The Stop-Light Diet for Children.* Boston and Toronto: Little, Brown, 1988.

Hall, Lindsey, and Leigh Cohn. *Bulimia: A Guide to Recovery.* Santa Barbara: Gurze Books, 1986.

Kinoy, Barbara, Estelle Miller, and John Atchley. *When Will We Laugh Again?* New York: Columbia University Press, 1984.

Lawrence, Marilyn, ed. *Fed Up and Hungry: Women, Oppression and Food.* New York: Peter Bedrick Books (by arrangement with The Women's Press Ltd., London), 1987.

Levenkron, Steven. *Treating and Overcoming Anorexia Nervosa.* New York: Charles Scribner's Sons, 1982; Warner paperback, 1983.

MacLeod, Sheila. *The Art of Starvation.* New York: Schocken Books, 1982.

Minuchin, Salvador, Bernice L. Rosman, and Lester Baker. *Psychosomatic Families: Anorexia Nervosa in Context.* Cambridge: Harvard University Press, 1978.

O'Neill, Cherry Boone. *Starving for Attention.* New York: Continuum, 1982.

Orbach, Susie. *Hunger Strike: The Anorectic's Struggle as a Metaphor for Our Age.* New York and London: W. W. Norton, 1986.

Roth, Geneen. *Feeding the Hungry Heart: The Experience of Compulsive Overeating.* Indianapolis and New York: Bobbs-Merrill, 1982.

Siegel, Michele, Judith Brisman, and Margot Weinshel. *Surviving an Eating Disorder: New Perspectives and Strategies for Family and Friends.* New York: Harper and Row, 1988.

Valette, Brett. *A Parent's Guide to Eating Disorders.* New York: Avon Books, 1988.

VIDEOTAPES

Faces of Recovery, narrated by Cathy Rigby McCoy. Cerritos, Calif.: College Health Enterprises, 1988. For information, contact Patricia Motz, R.N., Program Director, College Hospital, 10802 College Place, Cerritos, CA 90701 (213-924-9581; in California: 800-352-3301).

Focus: Eating Disorders. Kalamazoo, Mich.: Upjohn Company, Healthscope Series for the American College of Physicians. This public-service video is available through pharmacies. If your pharmacist does not have it, ask that it be ordered through the Upjohn representative.

ORGANIZATIONS

American Anorexia/Bulimia Association
418 East 76th Street
New York, NY 10021
(212-734-1114)

The National Anorectic Aid Society
1925 East Dublin Granville Road
Columbus, OH 43229
(Hotline: 614-436-1112, 8 A.M. to 5 P.M., Mon.–Fri.)

National Association of Anorexia Nervosa and Associated
Disorders (ANAD)
P. O. Box 7
Highland Park, IL 60035
(Hotline: 708-831-3438, 9 A.M. to 5 P.M., Mon.–Fri.)

Index